Restronguet Creek and Carrick Roads from a daffodil field above Penpol

AROUND THE FAL

Round Walks from Pendennis to Portscatho

Part of the view from the path between St Just and St Mawes, Walk 10. The rest is on the next three pages.

First published in this fully revised edition 2003
Original edition 1989, reprinted with revisions 1991& 1996
LANDFALL PUBLICATIONS
Landfall, Penpol, Devoran, Truro, Cornwall TR3 6NR

A CIP catalogue record for this book is available from the British Library.
ISBN 1 873443 46 3

Typesetting, illustrations and maps by Bob Acton except where indicated.

Printed by the Troutbeck Press and bound by R. Booth Ltd,
Antron Hill, Mabe, Penryn, Cornwall

ORDNANCE SURVEY MAPS

Most useful to walkers are the Explorer series (1:25,000). The one you will need is No.105 (Falmouth & Mevagissey).

COVER PHOTOGRAPHS

Front: The path beside Cowlands Creek, Walk 6
Back, top: Approaching St Just Creek, Walk 9
Back, bottom: Swans at Penpol, winter, Walks 4 & 5

Falmouth Harbour

Trefusis Point

INTRODUCTION

You would be hard put to it to find another region of similar size to the Fal estuary which offers so many beautiful, interesting and varied walks. There are few large areas which I was not able to include on any of the walks. The creekside between Trelissick and Feock, the Tregothnan estate, except the part around Lamorran, and the land west and south from Philleigh as far as Turnaware: these are comparatively inaccessible to walkers, but such areas remain almost totally "undeveloped" and thus form a marvellous backdrop to the walks on the opposite banks.

At the start of each walk description is an outline of the points of interest, together with practical advice on such matters as how to drive to the starting point, where to park, availability of refreshments en route, any special requirements such as waterproof footwear, and arrangements you could consider making beforehand to add to your enjoyment. Directions are given in bold type. In the directions, the circled paragraph numbers correspond with the numbered points on the sketch map for that walk.

To the best of my knowledge, all the routes are on public rights of way or permissive paths. Of course, things are always changing: a footbridge collapses, a farmer decides his cows will stray unless he puts up barbed wire, a new housing development is built ... With the help of readers, if they will let me know of any problems not mentioned in my directions, I will try to keep this book up-to-date as long as it remains in print, either by producing a small slip to insert, or by making more revisions in any further reprints that may be needed. For this latest edition, all the routes have been rewalked and revised as needed.

I hope you will enjoy doing these walks as much as my wife and 1 have, and if you arm yourself with the relevant O.S. map (see opposite) you will be able to make further discoveries for yourself.

Bob Acton

Percuil Creek (Walk 11)

MY THANKS TO ... Peter Gilson, a former teaching colleague and an authority on this region, who kindly checked through the whole text of the original edition and made many useful corrections and additions; Hilary Thompson, the well-known historian of the Roseland area, who vetted several walks in the 1996 edition; Phil Dyke, the National Trust's Country Manager for the Fal area, who read through parts of the text in 1995 and again in 2002 with special reference to NT sites; Andrew Pascoe for help with my sections on Pendennis and St Mawes Castles; Jeremy Williams of the Falmouth-Fowey Countryside Service, for much valuable advice and information; Ken Coad, who shared with me his knowledge and memories of the Ruan Lanihorne area; Mr A.M.Chart, Mrs J.George, Mr R.G.Williams, Mr D.Palmer, Mr R.G.Fautley, Mr Geof Purcell and Ms Barbara Tripp; the staff at the County Museum, Truro; Nick Johnson and Jeanette Ratcliffe of the Historic Environment Service (formerly the Cornwall Archaeological Unit). Finally, both my late wife, Viv, and my present wife, Stephanie, gave a fund of knowledge and ideas, and welcome company on the walks.

CONTENTS

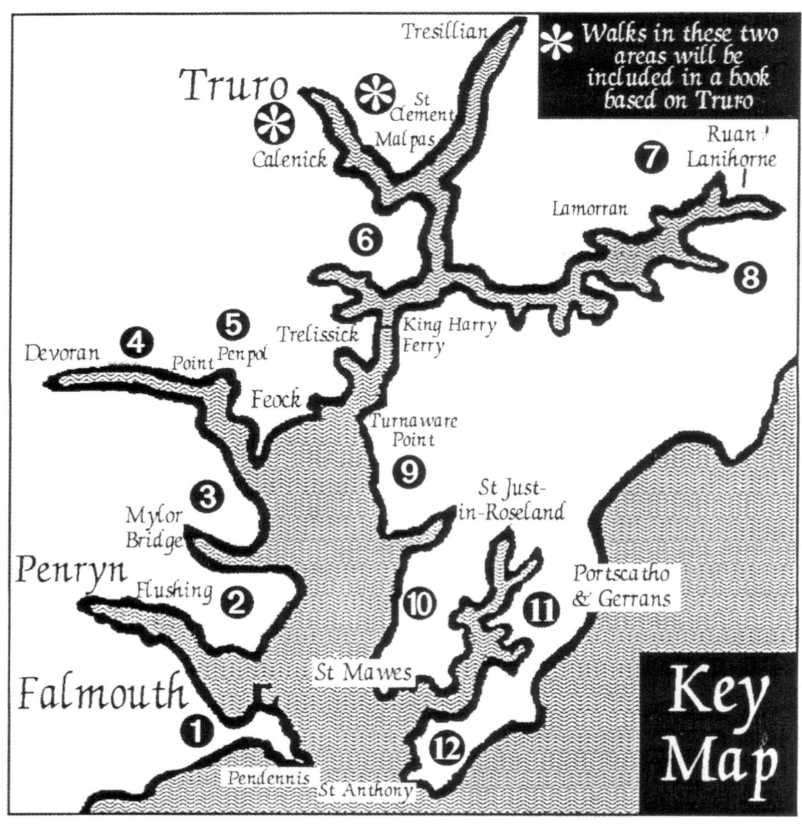

* Walks in these two areas will be included in a book based on Truro
Tresillian
Truro
St Clement
Malpas
Calenick
Ruan Lanihorne
Lamorran
Trelissick
King Harry Ferry
Devoran
Point
Penpol
Feock
Turnaware Point
St Just-in-Roseland
Mylor Bridge
Penryn
Flushing
Portscatho & Gerrans
St Mawes
Falmouth
Pendennis
St Anthony
Key Map

This one is for Cristabel:
not a great walker, but she does occasionally perambulate
Around our garden beside **the Fal**

Falling tide at Coombe, evening (Walk 6)

WALK 1

FALMOUTH DOCKS AND PENDENNIS POINT

About one and a half miles, or just over two if you include the suggested walk around the Castle moat

Note: A somewhat more detailed account of this walk is given in *Enjoy Falmouth and Around* (Landfall Publications, 1998). A recommended extension of the walk along the seafront to visit Gyllyngdune Gardens, which would add about a mile, and a possible further extension to Gyllyngvase and Swanpool, are described in that book. Two other walks exploring Falmouth and its history are also featured.

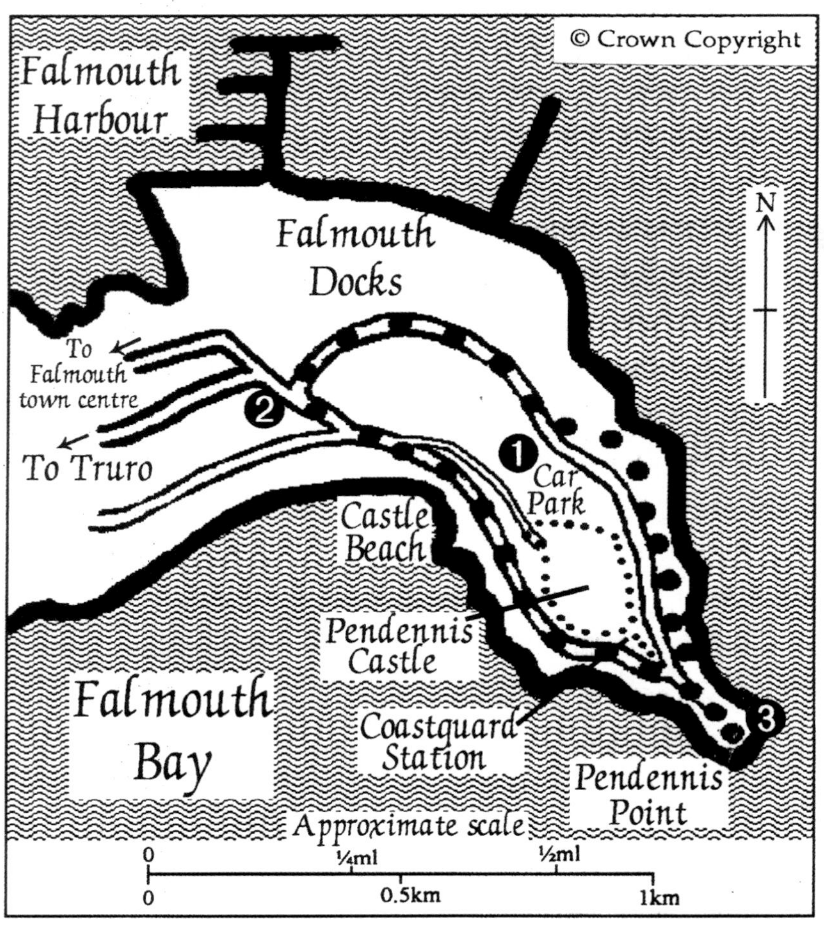

WALK 1

Even if you can spare only a morning or an afternoon you should have time to fit in, along with the short round walk, a visit to Pendennis Castle (opening hours: 1 April to 31 October, daily 10 am to 6 pm or dusk if earlier; rest of year, 10 am to 4 pm; phone 01326-316594 for current details). Even without visiting the Castle itself, you will see much evidence of fortifications mounted on the headland since Tudor times. We give information about many of them here, but if you want to know more I recommend an attractive leaflet, *Pendennis Headland Circular Walks,* produced by the Falmouth-Fowey Countryside Service.

The important Coastguard Station (strictly speaking, Falmouth Maritime Rescue Co-ordination Centre) is just south of the Castle, and visits to see the way things are run in the operations room can be arranged by telephoning the Station Officer, Operations (01326-212672). Such visits are normally restricted to groups.

On the walk you have an amazing bird's-eye view of Falmouth Docks; come on a working day if you can, to see ship-repair work in progress, and, if you are lucky, a ship being manoeuvred in or out of a dry dock. The walk around Pendennis Point provides magnificent views, firstly over Falmouth's beaches and along the coast beyond the Helford to the Manacles, and then, after you have reached the headland, of Carrick Roads and Falmouth Harbour. The seafront detour gives more fine views of Falmouth Bay, with an opportunity to relax on a beach if the tide is right, and refreshments are available during the season at the attractive Gyllyngdune Gardens, and in other cafés and hotels. A little road walking is involved, but there is always a footpath beside the road, and on the east side of Pendennis Point there is a well-walked path below the road level.

The directions are given from the free Pendennis Castle Car Park. The entrance to it is on Castle Drive, on the right not far beyond the viewing-point above Falmouth Docks. The other car park is for customers of the Ships & Castles Leisure Pool only: refreshments can be had in the Galley Restaurant there. This is normally open from 9 am to 7 pm, except on Sundays, when it closes at 4 pm. The Castle Car Park is further on along the one-way system (clockwise all around the Pendennis headland).

Close to the Ships & Castles complex stands a water tower; this substantial building, dating from 1905 and used until about the end of World War One to supply water to tented camps on the area known as the Hornwork, is worth inspecting. A plan exists to convert the tower into a viewpoint and exhibition centre.

WALK 1

Chambers' Dictionary defines a hornwork as "an outwork having angular points or horns, and composed of two demi-bastions joined by a curtain" (i.e. a rampart). The purpose of the Hornwork at Pendennis was to give extra defence on the landward side. It was built in 1627, and proved valuable during the Civil War when the castle was besieged. See page 9 in Peter Gilson's *Falmouth in Old Photographs* for an 18th-century engraving showing the Hornwork at that time. Little is left now: it fell into disrepair during the 19th century, leaving a flat, grassy area on which, in the following decades, were pitched the tents of militia units which came to the Pendennis garrison for annual training.

1 Walk back towards the Castle car park entrance. As you approach it, turn left along the footpath linking it to the Leisure Pool's car park. On reaching that, go right to join Castle Drive, the scenic road around the headland, constructed in 1865. **Turn left on Castle Drive, using the footpath at first, but cross soon** to see Falmouth Docks, and also a good view across the Inner Harbour to Falmouth and Trefusis Point.

The "Cutty Sark" in dry dock at Falmouth, 1938

FALMOUTH DOCKS

The foundation stone of the "New Docks" was laid in 1860, just three years before the arrival of the railway; the two together did much to relieve conditions in the town after a period of depression following the closure of the Post Office Packet Service in 1850. The only surviving large building from the original dockyard is the Grain Store, the four-storey stone building with two pitched roofs that stands on the extreme right, inland of the Eastern Breakwater. Of the four main dry docks (three of them currently in use), the largest, called Queen Elizabeth Dock, was opened in 1958, when the Docks were enjoying their most prosperous period. Designed to equip Falmouth to handle what were then the world's biggest vessels, it is 850 feet long, and can take ships up to 85,000 tons - less than one-tenth the size of the largest tankers of today. Until about the 1920s, ship building was a major activity at the Docks (198 vessels were built in all), but since then the work has consisted of repairing and refitting. Despite several crises in recent decades, which have seen a great reduction in the workforce, the Docks, with a good record of industrial relations and profitability, remain a vital part of the town's economy.

On the left side of the road here is part of a large oil-storage depot.

Continue along the road towards the imposing Falmouth Hotel, built on a narrow neck of land, so that its guests can enjoy views over both bay and harbour. The oldest of Falmouth's hotels specifically designed to accommodate holiday visitors (as distinct from the commercial hotels in the harbourside area, such as the Greenbank, King's and Royal), it was built, like Castle Drive, in 1865, just two years after the final section of the Cornwall Railway from Truro was completed, and its closeness to the railway terminus is no accident.

2 At the T-junction turn left, and then when you reach the coast road (Cliff Road), continue ahead towards the castle and Pendennis Point. If you wish to visit the castle go up the drive on the left beside the "No Entry" signs.

PENDENNIS CASTLE

"Pendennis" means "Castle Headland"; the name goes back well before 1539, when Henry VIII decreed that castles should be built here, at St Mawes, at Trefusis Point and at Gyllyngdune. A map made in 1540 shows an ancient rampart at the neck of the headland; it also shows that work on St Mawes Castle had started, but not yet at Pendennis. However, both castles were complete by 1546; the plans for Trefusis and Gyllyngdune were dropped. The theory was that since "Black Rock", at the entrance to the harbour, obliged entering ships to steer towards either Pendennis or St Mawes, the guns at those two castles would be able to defend the harbour adequately. (An alternative explanation is that they simply ran out of money!) To defend the Castle against attack from the north, it was surrounded by a four-acre enclosure with steep walls, embrasures for more guns and a dry moat in the years after 1598. In 1627 the Hornwork was added. When it was besieged during the Civil War (1646) it held out for five months and eventually surrendered only because of famine; the Governor, Sir John Arundell, and his garrison of 900 were allowed to march out with honours. In the 20th century the castle was

occupied by the army as part of the coastal defences during both World Wars. Pendennis has been described by Nick Johnson, the County Archaeologist, as "a gem of military architecture" which "has reflected every major foreign policy change since Tudor times." Apart from the buildings themselves and the magnificent views to be had, attractions for visitors include a museum with a good collection of weapons and armour, and annual re-enactments of events in the Castle's history. One of the more modern buildings within the Castle complex - dating from 1901, when barracks were built for the 105 Battery, Royal Garrison Artillery - is now used as a Café and Youth Hostel - surely among the best-situated YHA facilities in the country!

To continue the walk go on along the road till you reach Pendennis Point. The first path down on the right, leading to a shelter, continues a short way along the cliff edge and then returns to the road. The two paths that come later lead down to the foreshore - a good place to study rock pools. On these rocks during the years between the World Wars lay the rusting remains of five German submarines, broken up for scrap in World War 2.

A recently reopened path, known as Hunters' Path, (steep and possibly

slippery in places) runs among the Evergreen Oaks and Monterey Pines on the slope to your left, which is the western side of the hill on which the castle stands. The hillside was landscaped by officers stationed at the castle in the 19th century, who wanted to make a park of it, complete with garden, a grotto and an arboretum. Work has recently been done to restore the officers' paths and grotto. The main path runs beside at least two small quarries from which stone for the Castle was obtained. Where the path rejoins the road there is a little "island", said to mark the site of a smuggler's grave. The remains of the grotto are close to the road a short way north of that (so if you want to see it you need to turn right along the road on leaving Hunters' Path).

Where the road curving round the headland reaches the car park on the Point, the drive up to Falmouth Coastguard Station is on the left.

Falmouth is one of six Coastguard Maritime Rescue Co-ordination Centres in Britain; the others are at Swansea, Clyde, Aberdeen, Yarmouth and Dover. To quote from an official leaflet: "Rescue Centres keep a constant radio watch on the international distress frequencies and also handle telephone, telex and facsimile messages through specially designed consoles. Each Centre has a fully fitted operations room with emergency planning, press and staff facilities, along with storage for rescue equipment, vehicles and boats." The Falmouth Centre covers the coastline from Tintagel to Dodman Point, and 650,000 square miles of sea, as far as 15°W longitude, and can communicate with ships anywhere in the world via the Inmarsat satellite system. (An interesting example which occurred early in 1998 was when no-one in the world except Falmouth coastguards responded to a distress signal from four Ukrainian sailors who had for six months been trapped in the Suez Canal without supplies or cash on an abandoned ship.)

Even if you don't have an appointment to visit the Coastguard Station, it's well worth going up the drive in order to get on to the path which goes around the castle moat - a delightful walk with superb views, and it also gives a close-up of the Castle's outer defences. **Continue past the entrance to the Coastguard Station, and where the track curves left go straight on through the zigzag gap in the fence and along the narrow path, which soon brings you out on top of the bank surrounding the moat. Where this curves left beside the Hornwork car park, the path along the top becomes narrow and rather unstable-looking, so (unless you want to return to your car now) it's best to go down the steps into the moat and follow it around three sides of the Castle until you reach the Castle entrance gate.**

There are several protrusions or "bastions" in the steep outer wall, best seen from the bottom of the moat, installed to make defence easier against any attacker by giving "enfillade fire", that is, fire from the side. The moat never held water; instead, a line of pointed wooden stakes once ran all the way along the centre of it. It is not complete today, having been filled in its south-east corner to allow the construction of a special gun emplacement in 1894.

Continue along the moat, passing beneath the Castle entrance before returning to the higher-level path.

At the moat's southern extremity, the well-preserved double gun emplacement, used in both the World Wars, is known as Half Moon Battery.

HALF MOON BATTERY

This crescent-shaped platform was created in 1795 as hard standing for cannons, and for the next 161 years - apart from a gap of just over a year in 1938-9 - Half Moon Battery was equipped with long-range guns. During World War 2 the Battery was armed with two 6-inch Mark 7 Breech Loading Guns which were used against enemy vessels on several occasions, mainly targeting "E" Boats with radar assistance. In 1956 the Battery was dismantled and the guns were cut up for scrap. Two six-inch guns were brought here from Shoeburyness in 1995. This was only a small part of an ambitious programme undertaken jointly by English Heritage and Carrick District Council to restore and open to the public coastal defence works of all periods at Pendennis. Unfortunately, Half Moon Battery is accessible only to paying visitors to the castle, although you can see it pretty well from the paths.

Rejoin the track or road passing the Coastguard Station entrance and retrace your steps back to Castle Drive. Out on Pendennis Point, beyond the car park, it's worth going down on the east (harbour) side to look at Little Dennis Blockhouse.

LITTLE DENNIS BLOCKHOUSE

Little Dennis seems to have been built a few years before the castle itself as part of a defensive site - few vestiges of which remain - covering the whole of the southern end of the headland. The blockhouse appears originally to have been armed with one or more cannon on the roof; others were sited just to the north. Notice how, as on the Castle, the battlements lean inwards to lessen the impact of shot. Inside, you can see the holes which once carried the big

Little Dennis. Black Rock and St Anthony Lighthouse in the distance

beam supporting the roof; the fireplace and oven show that the garrison actually lived and fed here - and how very uncomfortable that must have been in winter!

3 From there, I suggest you take the footpath which runs along the cliff edge and then turns inland around two small inlets known in Cornwall as "zawns", from the Cornish *sawn*, a cleft or gully; the same word explains the name of Zone Point, near St Anthony. **(If, however, you find this path difficult, retrace your steps to Castle Drive, turning right and returning to the car park that way.)**

From the path, the opening on the right leads to the remains of an old quay (Crab Quay) and a gun emplacement; bear left of this. (It's worth at least a brief inspection first, though. The quay is one of the very few landing stages on the headland. Like Half Moon, the gun emplacement was created in 1795. Its original purpose was probably as a defence against vessels close inshore which the Castle guns could not depress sufficiently to attack. From 1902-6 it was used to provide cover for a submarine minefield across the harbour entrance. After that it was abandoned until 1940, when two 6-pounder guns were installed as a defence against motor torpedo boats. As a result of recent restoration work it is once again quite clear where the guns were mounted, and the magazine building and a small storehouse have survived at the rear of the site. There are also five searchlight platforms on the rocks below the battery.)

Late in 1995 the Enys estate was one of four sites shortlisted as the campus for the proposed University of Cornwall, but in the event Tremough, on the edge of Penryn, was chosen.

You cross a small stream on re-entering woodland after a relatively open section. Where a lane crosses, go left then immediately right through the first of many tiny iron gates which do duty instead of stiles in this district. Continue ahead beside the hedge on the right. After the next little gate (from which there is a long view behind to the china-clay area near St Austell) **go on in the same direction; cross the drive and follow the yellow arrow by the left-hand granite post.** Now you can get a glimpse of Pendennis Castle almost straight ahead. **The path - narrow and sometimes rather overgrown at first - goes to the right of Gwarder farm, via more small gates. Next, keep by the hedge on the left, and continue along the often muddy farm lane past Pencoose farmhouse and outbuildings.** (*Coose* or *goose* in Cornish place names refers to a wood.) **Eventually the lane brings you down to a road at the edge of Penryn.**

You are now at Round Ring, the site of an Iron Age hill settlement, though little if any evidence of it remains beyond the name and a few curved field boundaries which suggest there was once quite a large circular rampart enclosing a smaller central ring.

This area is called Bohelland, although in fact several early documents use the name, with many variations such as Behethlan, Betheldan and Behellan, to refer to St Gluvias parish as a whole. (The last syllable derives from the Cornish *lann*, meaning enclosed cemetery or church-site.) The so-called "Bohelland Tragedy" was first recounted in a pamphlet published in 1618. Its lengthy title neatly sums up what happened: "a most bloody and unexampled Murther very lately committed by a Father on his own Sonne (who was lately returned from the Indyes) at the instigation of a merciless Step-mother." The grisly tale was made into a very effective play recently by Donald Rawe, but if you missed that and want to know all the details, a quite lengthy version of it is given in Lake's Parochial History (Vol. 3, pages 87-8).

4 Turn left and then after 25 yards take the footpath on the right. Continue down Bohelland Rise. At the T-junction cross the road, keep to the right of the main block of garages, and go on down the path where it resumes. This brings you out opposite the Volvo showrooms.

5 Turn left on the high pavement of this road. Soon you reach St Gluvias Church.

WALK 2
ST GLUVIAS CHURCH

St Gluvias is the parish church of Penryn - more accurately, most of Penryn, since part is in Budock parish, with which St Gluvias was united till last century. Standing as it does at the head of Penryn Creek (or, in other words, at the limit of the navigable part of the Penryn River), it appears to mark the site of one of the earliest Celtic settlements around here. Parts of the church - notably the tower - date from the 15th century, but most of the old structure was rebuilt in the 18th century, and much of what still remained of the medieval church was destroyed during a harsh restoration in 1883. According to Sheila Bird, another bit was lost when French sailors took the main door to replace the rudder of their ship.

St Gluvias Church, Penryn, in the snow

When you are ready to walk on, go back a few yards down the road to where the waterside path begins, near the metal gates at the entrance to Islington Wharf. To your right across the river are the boatyards and old warehouses of Penryn, with its clock tower and granite houses.

WALK 2
PENRYN

Penryn is one of Cornwall's oldest towns, granted its charter in 1265, long before Falmouth was anything more than a word on maps, denoting the harbour. Almost nothing is left of Glasney, the great Collegiate Church dissolved in 1547, but there are still plenty of old buildings, many of them beautifully restored since 1975, when Penryn became a Housing Action Area because so much of the older part of the town had deteriorated to the level of a slum. Falmouth's rise helped to cause the decline of Penryn, and there is still much rivalry between the two. From the Exchequer Quay tin, granite and oysters were shipped, and imports included cattle from Spain. (As with Falmouth and Truro, an adequate note on Penryn would at least double the size of this book, and since I'm aiming to produce something easily portable it's better to refer you to the Further Reading list.)

After Penryn Quay come the modern industrial buildings along the Penryn-Falmouth road.

Before long the path passes through St Gluvias' overflow graveyard. At the first inlet, Sailor's Creek, arrows direct you down to the foreshore, where a small wooden footbridge helps you to negotiate a marshy, reed-filled area. Later you come to metal gates, with Trevissome House to your left and Falmouth Marina on the far shore. Then comes your first sight of Falmouth Docks with Pendennis Castle behind. At the next inlet, with its clutch of houseboats, you have a small stream to cross, and just beyond that the path can at times be very boggy, but if this proves a problem you can walk at a higher level.

6 As you approach the boatyard at Little Falmouth, go up to the left, where there is a rather high and awkward stile to cross. After negotiating that take the path on your right, follow round to the left behind the Falmouth Boat Company yard and up the slope.

LITTLE FALMOUTH

Once there was a pilchard processing plant at Little Falmouth, but since the late 17th century it has been a shipbuilding and repair yard. The first dry dock in the harbour was built here in 1820. The yard produced several ships for the Royal Navy and the Falmouth Packet service during the early 19th century. Sheila Bird gives details of several notable vessels from later years, including the Charlotte Padbury, which when launched in 1874 was said to be the largest barque built in Cornwall. Today, many RNLI lifeboats are serviced here.

7 Turn right at the road, passing St Peter's Church and the first of Flushing's two pubs, the Royal Standard. At the right bend that brings you to the main street beside the harbour, notice a warning sign that must surely be unique: SLOW - SWANS CROSSING. Soon comes the other pub, the Seven Stars. According to *History Around the Fal* Part III "the Seven Stars was built on a beach, which was under water at high tides". This was around the middle of the 18th century, so it would seem that the whole main street, or at least this end of it, was foreshore then. The present building, dating from about 1908, was raised by three feet.

FLUSHING

Since at least as far back as the Norman Conquest, the Lords of the Manor in this area had been the Trefusis family. "Trefusis" means "fortified place", presumably a true reflection of the precautions required against seafaring marauders in such an exposed spot; and Trefusis Point was originally chosen by Henry VIII as one of four sites for castles to defend Penryn, Truro and the other ports up-river, but later it was decided that two were adequate. Maps from the late 16th century show a house called "Nankersis" (probably meaning "valley of the reed swamp") south west of Trefusis, and with the growth of Falmouth more dwellings were built there, because it was the best point for a ferry crossing, linking Falmouth with Truro via Mylor, Restronguet Passage and Calenick. About 1660, Francis Trefusis decided to emulate Sir Peter Killigrew's success in creating and promoting Falmouth by hiring Dutch engineers, experts in land drainage and the construction of sea walls, to develop the hamlet of Nankersey into a rival port. The quay walls they built used no mortar, and this broke the force of waves by allowing the water to penetrate; probably that is why the walls have survived in good condition. Many of the attractive, slate-hung houses in the village were built for the Dutchmen. They called their temporary home after the place many of them came from, Vlissingen, and although they didn't stay many years the English version of that name has stuck. Francis's son, Samuel Trefusis, tried to get the Post Office Packet Service transferred from Falmouth to Flushing; he failed (partly, no doubt, because his forebears had supported the Parliamentary cause during the Civil War), but he did bring it about that all officers and crew of Packet ships must live in Flushing, and that brought prosperity and an air of elegance and sophistication for a short time to the village as well as increasing the Trefusis family fortune. By the end of the 18th century Flushing was becoming a popular holiday resort, partly because of its mild climate. It depends heavily on tourism now, but traditional occupations like boatbuilding, oyster dredging and fishing are still carried on.

Greenbank, Falmouth, as seen from above the quay at Flushing

Linger on the quay for a while: it affords a fine view of Falmouth harbour and of Flushing's waterside houses. Then **continue along the main street and follow the road round to the left out of the village, still skirting the water's edge.** There is another magnificent view at the corner; and it's worth turning left just after the corner to visit the Bowling Green, now a small park, which commands an impressive panorama. Notice the small quarry at the corner. It is said that before the present road was built the quarry was open to the sea, and boats could enter to pick up stone.

On the site of the house called Carn-Du (on the right not far past the quarry) was once a silver-lead mine. This was Wheal Clinton, active during the 1850s, when a 24-inch beam engine was brought from a mine in Gwennap parish to drain the levels, which ran both inland and under the estuary. The mine closed in 1858 because of fears that the sea would break in, but the engine house remained for about another thirty years, and a photograph of it c.1880 is included in Hamilton Jenkin's *Mines and Miners of Cornwall*, Part 13. It can also be seen in the distance in an old engraving reproduced in *Enjoy Falmouth*.

8 Where Trefusis Road ends, you may care to go down on the right to Kiln Beach and Kiln Quay, named after a long-vanished limekiln; but **to continue**

the walk take the main track straight ahead. On the right immediately beyond the track down to the foreshore is a large black-and-white half-timbered house named Kiln Quay. This - or at any rate most of it - is modern, having been rebuilt following a fire, but the original building was, we believe, a genuine Tudor house transported from south-east England!

Continue through the trees and over the cattle-grid on to Trefusis Point. The path now skirts the edge of the low cliff, presenting you with several stiles and, in normal Cornish weather, plenty of mud at gates. Towards the end of the very dry summer of 1995, however, all was bone dry, and a large area of furze (the usual term for gorse in Cornwall) had been destroyed by fire. It was just starting to show signs of regeneration by the end of August.

Where the shore curves west towards Mylor at Penarrow Point, notice the obelisk on the beach, inscribed T.B., meaning Truro Boundary. The line from here to Messack Point, near St Just, marks the boundary between Truro and Falmouth Harbours, and every six years the ceremony of beating the bounds takes place, when the Mayor, Corporation and Harbourmaster of Truro visit the obelisks at Penarrow and Messack. (Messack Point is visited on Walk 9.)

After the Restronguet Sailing Club you pass among houses before reaching Mylor Dockyard with its marina for pleasure boats, recently greatly enlarged. A small restaurant here, The Ganges, opens only during the season, but there is now (2002) also a café, which was open on a January Sunday when I was last there.

MYLOR DOCKYARD

During the Napoleonic Wars the Admiralty built a dock at Mylor in order to supply provisions to the fleet, since Falmouth was too busy dealing with the Packets. The dock was busy again during the Crimean War. The Ganges restaurant was named after the Naval Training Ship - notorious for the harsh treatment inflicted on trainees - which was berthed nearby from 1866 to 1899. During World War 2 the yard was used by French resistance fighters, and by U.S. troops at the time of the Normandy landings.

9 Just past the phone box, go through the gate into Mylor churchyard, then up past the church, through the lych gate, and take the track on the other side of the road, between a house and a bungalow. Here you get a good view of Mylor Creek. **Continue along the road which follows the water's edge, passing the little creek at Trelew. Later, a signed footpath on the right gives access to the foreshore at Tregatreath; if you decide to go that way you can return to the road via a short lane that starts beside a boatyard.**

WALK 2
MYLOR CHURCH AND CHURCHYARD

Mylor Church has a special place in my affections as the home for many years of a little annual music festival (featuring musicians of the calibre of Roger Norrington) which eventually developed into the Three Spires Festival, based at Truro Cathedral. By the time orchestra, chorus and soloists were packed in, there was little room for an audience in the tiny Norman church, so many stood listening at the open doors on those balmy evenings when summers really were summers... But in any weather this is an idyllic spot. The graveyard has the tallest ancient cross in Cornwall (though some of its 17½ feet are buried) and also some of the most-quoted gravestone inscriptions in the County. I'll leave you to find for yourself the memorials to Joseph Crapp and Thomas James (shot, thanks to the "officious zeal" of a customs officer), along with the graves of numerous shipwreck victims, especially those from the Queen transport, wrecked on Trefusis Point, and also the Ganges memorial to a distressingly large number of boys who died on the training ship anchored off St Just.

10 At the crossroads follow the sign to Mylor Bridge.

On the right now is the George VI Playing Field, created early in the 1950s from what was formerly marshland. A stile gives access to it, and **you can if you wish cross the playing field to the stepping stones across the creek,** said to mark the point where a dam was built to create a reservoir for the tide mill mentioned near the start of Walk 3. **If the tide is low enough for you to cross, a path on the other side will bring you to Trevellan Road, close to the Post Office; turn left then right for the village car park. If not, continue ahead, and at the main road bear right over the bridge to return to the car park.**

SOME ALTERNATIVE ROUTES, MOSTLY SHORTER

TO START AT MYLOR

Coming from the main car park, walk or drive over the bridge at the head of the creek and take the first left turning, and then first left again, Church Road. There is usually room to park at the start of this road; if you start the walk here, it will be about five miles in length. Continue along the creekside road for about half a mile, and just as you approach a small inlet (Trelew Creek), take the signed public footpath on the right. Go through the first farm gate, marked Trelew farm, but just before the second one turn left through a small wooden gate; keep right where the path divides, and then pass through a 5-bar gate marked "Footpath". Now follows a very pretty but sometimes very wet path beside a tiny stream. When you emerge into an open field, keep to the right-hand side. A stile brings you to a road; turn left on it. Go straight on at the crossroads. Immediately after the cattle-grid cross the stile on the right; bear left to another stile, and then keep to the right-hand edge of the field. This brings you to the outskirts of Flushing. Go down the road and turn left at the bottom. Now follow the directions from section 7 (starting immediately after the note about Flushing) to return to your starting-place.

TO START AT FLUSHING

If you need to park your car, your best bet is to drive on through the main street and round the corner on to Trefusis Road; there is usually room to park along there. Now follow the directions from point 8, turning left on to the path just after Trelew Creek if you want the shortest route (about 4 miles in all), as described above. If you have arrived from Falmouth on the ferry and want a walk, simply turn right from the quay and start with direction 7 (beginning immediately after the note about Flushing); you could then do four miles by turning back at Trelew, eight miles by going on to Enys and Penryn, or even twelve miles by linking up with Walk 3.

WALK 3

MYLOR BRIDGE, GREATWOOD, THE PANDORA & HALWYN

About five and a half miles.
A shorter walk, omitting the Pandora and Halwyn,
is suggested in section 3. This is about three miles in length.

The shorter of our two walks based on Mylor continues the path round the beautiful western shores of Carrick Roads and into the equally lovely Restronguet Creek. Apart from Mylor itself there are no villages on this section, and few houses - just the occasional one standing in enviable (I tried hard to avoid 'splendid'!) isolation, and small clusters around Greatwood, Restronguet Weir and Restronguet Passage. Refreshments are available there, at the famous Pandora Inn. There are also shops and the Lemon Arms at Mylor. The walking is easy, apart from a steepish hill after Halwyn; the path is well-walked and should be fairly dry underfoot. Towards the end there is an unfortunately unavoidable quarter-mile-or-so on a road which can be moderately busy. A suggestion on how to link this walk with Walk 2 is given in italics at the start of point 6, making one round walk of over twelve miles: a good day out, but not too exhausting if you're reasonably fit.

The map for this walk, plus instructions for driving to Mylor Bridge and comments on parking there, are at the start of Walk 2.

1 From the car park, turn right down the main village street, Lemon Hill, for a few yards.

Notice the small clock tower on the left, dating from 1845; it was a gift from Sir Charles Lemon, the grandson of the William Lemon mentioned in the later note on Carclew. The building behind the clock was originally the parish workhouse and was converted as a school in 1850 by Sir Charles Lemon. In 1921 it suffered a serious fire, and a new school building (seen on Walk 2) was provided. Finally the old poor house became the Tremayne Hall, whose name recalls another benefactor of the village: the Tremaynes succeeded the Lemons as owners of Carclew. Tremayne Hall is now the meeting-place for most village groups (WI, Darby & Joan Club, Mylor Players, and more). The bridge ahead, from which the village takes its name, was till 1950 wide enough only for a farm cart. The village smithy used to stand on the left, just this side of the bridge. On a more practical note, the public loos are just the other side of it!

Take the left turning before the bridge, Trevellan Road.

Several house names on the left side of Trevellan Road indicate that a watermill stood here. "Trevellan" includes a version of the Cornish word for a mill, "melin", and the quay at the end is called Mill Quay. One of the houses features a millstone now doing duty as a sundial. Two mills belonging to Restronguet Manor were in existence by 1417. "New Mill" is shown on this site on Boazio's map of the Fal, 1597, and "two grist mills called Restronguet Mills" are mentioned in a lease of 1771. One of them was probably a tide mill created by the construction of an embankment across the head of the creek to impound water at high tide. The other was powered by a leat which, as mentioned at the start of Walk 2, ran where the village car park now is; it continued along what is now Tremayne Close.

Notice the royal coat of arms on Quay House, the last house on the right; we wondered if this was the Customs House, but its owner told us he owns the coat of arms and puts it up on every house he lives in!

Continue along Mylor Creek, following the signs to Greatwood and Restronguet. Where the road bends left, go straight on along the narrow path, and at the breeze-block wall follow round to the left, entering the field by the metal gate. Old OS maps show Limekiln Quay on the foreshore below at this point; whether anything remains of the kiln I don't know. The path crosses the field, heading back to the creekside.

2 At the gate - one of many "kissing gates" on this walk - you can continue walking along the field edge, or go along the foreshore, returning to the path at the little inlet, immediately inland from which is a small disused quarry. Later the path runs along a short causeway across marshy ground at another small inlet, where there appear to be slight remains of an old quay. A farm lane runs inland from this inlet, and the quay may have been useful for landing supplies of seaweed and sand for the fields. As you reach the end of this small peninsula you pass through a stretch of the path famous for its spring flowers - a riot of primroses, celandines, violets, and especially daffodils. The small quay is known as Greatwood Quay; from here there was once a ferry service to the other side of Mylor Creek. The view is splendid, with Mylor Docks and Boatyard to the right, St Just-in-Roseland opposite, and a glimpse of Trelissick far left.

3 At the signpost you have a choice of ways:

For the short walk, turn left along a quiet country road, as directed for Restronguet Barton. After about a quarter of a mile you have a fine view to the left at the sharp-right corner, and further glimpses to the right after that. Continue for another half mile. Soon after passing Restronguet Barton you reach a T-junction; here turn left, and where the

right-hand edge of the scene are the big buildings of Wheal Jane, just below the skyline. The farmland and woods in the foreground are mostly the Carclew estates.

CARCLEW

The great house of Carclew, overlooking Restronguet Creek, was built in 1728 for Samuel Kempe, a gentleman from Penryn who had married into the Bonython family, owners of Carclew Barton. In 1749 it was bought, together with its deer park, gardens and plantations covering more than a square mile, by William Lemon, who had made a vast fortune, mainly from the copper mines. (His name is perpetuated in Lemon Street and Lemon Quay, Truro, as well as Lemon Hill and the Lemon Arms at Mylor Bridge, though the last two allude to his grandson, Charles. You can read more about the Lemon family in Viv Acton's "A History of Truro", Volume 1.) Carclew House was burnt down in 1934, and little remains except part of the Ionic façade. The splendid gardens, famous for their rhododendrons, lily pond and lake, are occasionally opened to the public: during 2003, every Sunday afternoon in April and May, except Easter. For up-to-date details, ring 01872-864070, or see the annual "Cornwall Gardens" leaflet, published by the Cornwall Tourist Board.

There is no public right of way through the Carclew grounds, so here we have one of only three short stretches between Falmouth and Truro where there is no public footpath or road beside the water. (The others are between Feock and Trelissick, and between another Halwyn, near Old Kea, and Truro.)

6 At the road, turn left, unless you would like to do Walk 2 now instead of returning immediately to Mylor. In that case, turn right, then take the next left turning. Where this road is joined by a slightly busier one from the right, bear left. About a quarter of a mile later, turn right at the first surfaced road (Broads Lane). Now follow the directions for Walk 2, starting at point 2 (page 18).

Whichever way you go, you need to take special care to watch for fast traffic on this narrow road.

Continuing now with the directions for the last part of Walk 3:

7 For the most direct way back to Mylor Bridge you could go down Bell's Hill - that is, keep right where the road forks. Unless you are tired, however, or late for a very important date, I recommend you to take the left fork, signed to Weir and Restronguet. This is much quieter than Bell's Hill, and runs through pleasant woodland. Here and there you have good views to the right, with Penryn in the middle distance and the tower of Mabe church on the skyline a little further left.

8 **At the crossroads, you again have the option of turning right for Mylor, this time down Passage Hill, but I suggest you still continue ahead.**

An unusual memorial beside the road was erected in gratitude by Ukrainian refugees from Russian Communism who found a home in this district soon after World War 2.

9 **Where the road bends left at Restronguet Barton** - the site of Restronguet Manor House, though little if anything seems to have survived of the original building - **turn right through a metal farm gate, then over a stone stile beside a public footpath sign to Mylor Bridge. Keep beside the hedge on your left. The last part of this path runs between hedges** and looks like a typical old pack-horse lane - in this case linking Restronguet Manor and its farm with the manor mills and the quay.

On reaching the quay, retrace your steps at the start of the walk to return to the car park.

WALK 4

DEVORAN, POINT & PENPOL
with a possible extension to FEOCK

About 3 miles, or about 6 miles including Feock

Note: This account is based on parts of Walks 14 and 15 in *Exploring Cornwall's Tramway Trails* Volume 2. Please refer to that book for detailed information about such topics as the County Adit, the Gwennap mining district and ancilliary industries such as the Perran Foundry and the mineral railway (the Redruth & Chasewater Railway).

This is a very fine walk in terms of both scenery and historical interest. Those who have enjoyed discovering the remains of the mineral railway between Redruth and Devoran will want to follow it to its southern terminus at Point Quay, and the visit to Feock includes a look at Pill Creek, one of the places from which copper ore was shipped to South Wales before the railway was built. Other "industrial archaeology" en route includes visible relics of tin streaming, three underwater mines, a well-preserved limekiln, a smelting works and a tide-operated bone mill. Among many other points of interest are a pretty village green and a medieval church.

Much of the route is on minor roads, but some of the paths and tracks are liable to be muddy. There is no source of provisions along the way except the pub in Devoran.

To drive to Devoran from Truro, take the A39 south towards Falmouth. At the end of the Carnon Downs bypass you reach the main turning to Devoran on the left, but continue a little further, past the Bissoe turning (right). Take the next turning left, and where this road turns left into the village, go straight on for a few yards, into Quay Road. You should find parking space here, either beside the road on the right, or in a space on the left. If not, roadside parking elsewhere in the village should be possible.

The start/end point for the walk is the foot of Market Street, where it meets Greenbank Road and Quay Road.

DEVORAN

The name means "waters": very apt, since here three streams (the Carnon River, the Kennall and the Trewedna stream) meet the tidal waters of Restronguet (or Devoran) Creek - though in fact the Carnon River was tidal and even, it is said, navigable once as far as Bissoe Bridge.

It is scarcely an exaggeration to state that Devoran owes its very existence

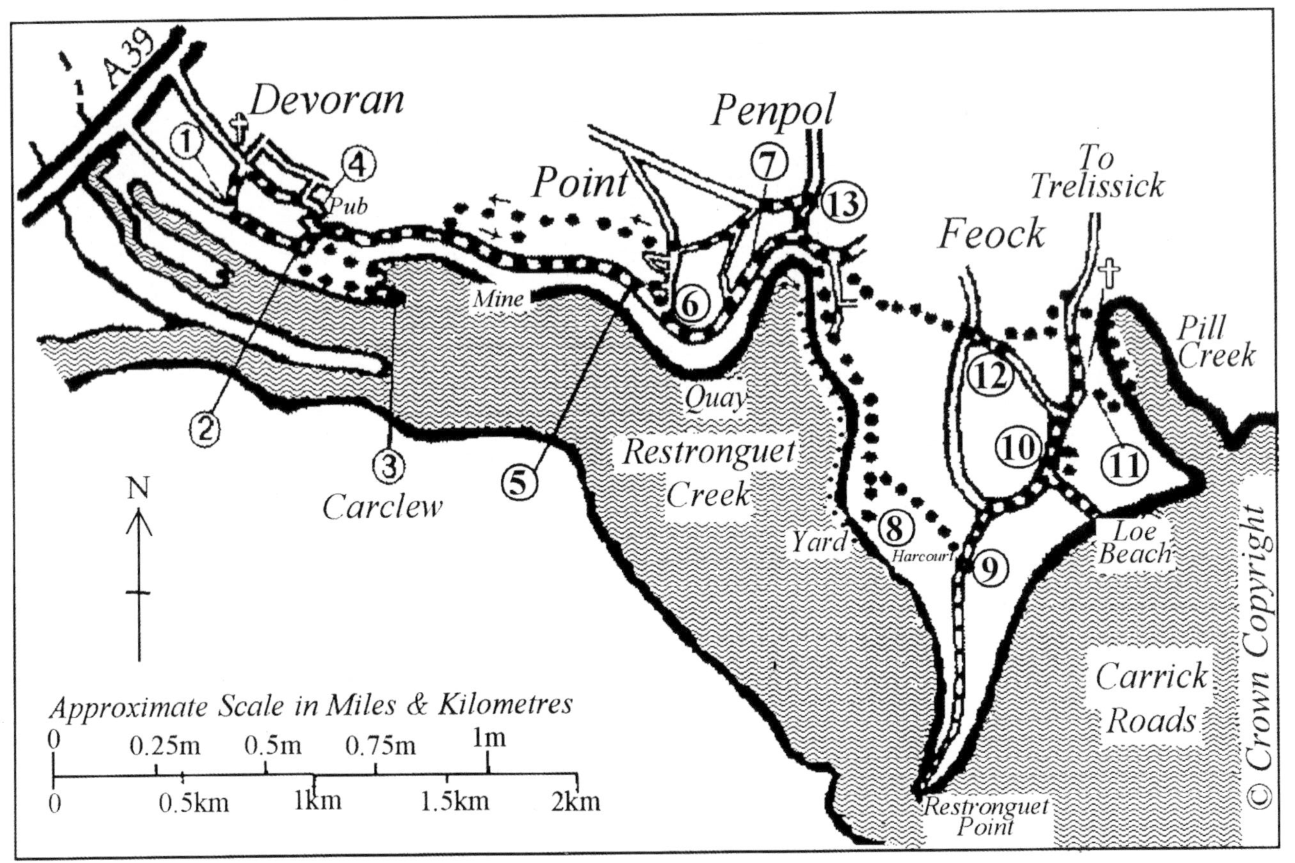
A39
Devoran
Pub
Point
Penpol
To
Trelissick
Feock
Pill
Creek
Mine
Quay
Restronguet
Creek
Carclew
Yard
Harcourt
Loe
Beach
Carrick
Roads
Restronguet
Point
© Crown Copyright
1
2
3
4
5
6
7
8
9
10
11
12
13
N
Approximate Scale in Miles & Kilometres
0 0.25m 0.5m 0.75m 1m
0 0.5km 1km 1.5km 2km

to the Redruth & Chasewater Railway and the docks built by the railway company. The first edition Ordnance Survey map (1813) indicates nothing besides Lower Devoran Farm on the site. The 1841 census (17 years after the coming of the railway) gives the population of the village as 250, and by 1871 it had risen to 1500. Nowadays, even small pleasure boats have to pick their moment carefully to get up to Devoran without scraping the bottom, and yet not much over a century ago it was among the most important ports in Cornwall, exporting vast tonnages of copper ore from the Gwennap mines for smelting in South Wales, and importing coal from there and timber from Scandinavia for the mines. (It has been claimed that the equivalent of 300 square miles of Norwegian forest was underground in Cornwall in the middle of the 19th century.)

1 The walk begins by going along Quay Road, but first I suggest you walk a few yards along Greenbank Road, as far as the entrance to the Devoran Boatyard, the first turning on the left.

Greenbank Road runs between the old Redruth & Chasewater Railway track - which ran just this side of the older houses on the right - and the foreshore of Devoran Creek, to your left. Much of this part of the foreshore is now occupied by industrial buildings. One of the many railway sidings which ran to the quays lining the foreshore went along the left side of what is now the boatyard entrance: 14 setts (granite blocks to which the rails were attached) can still be seen.

Return to the junction with Market Street.

Notice, in the garden on the left at the corner, the posts of a level-crossing gate, not quite in their original position now. The line itself ran parallel with Carclew Terrace, a few feet away from the houses.

Continue ahead along Quay Road.

Just past the foot of Market Street the line divided into three. The branch to the left ran beside the wall along the left side of what is now a parking space, passed to the left of the workshops (now the Devoran Village Hall) and continued beside the creek as a horse-drawn tramway for about a mile and a half to Point and Penpol. The one on the right ran along what is now Quay Road, with many sidings to quays on the right, and ended at what is now known as Devoran Quay. The short spur between them served the workshop and the engine shed beyond it.

Some of the older buildings on the left on Quay Road are relics of the railway: as already mentioned, the Village Hall originated as the workshops, and the attractive Old Quay House, with the picture of the loco named Spitfire at its gate, was once the Company's offices. The large house now called Hazeldene was formerly the Crown & Anchor Hotel. The start of one of the sidings appears to be revealed in the parking space in front of the bungalow on the right called Smelter's Rest, named after another loco.

2 Where the road makes a double hairpin-bend up to the Old Quay Inn, take the narrow path bearing right on to Devoran Quay.

DEVORAN QUAY

A fine job has been done during the past few years by the Devoran Quay Preservation Society in restoring much of the quay to something close to its original form. On your right when you first walk out on to the quay are the upper parts of what was once a complex system of wharves and docks, now gardens and bungalows. Downriver, only one modern building has encroached on the quay area, a bungalow which stands on the site of a loco shed. On the waterfront side of it are the ruins of eight of the original twelve "hutches" in which copper ore was stored ready for shipment to South Wales. The railway line ran on a wooden structure behind them, level with the tops of the walls (then about 10-12ft high), so that the ore could be tipped in. It was transferred to the ships by barrow, although horses were used to haul wagons along the numerous sidings to the quayside.

A sketch based on an old photo: Devoran Quay in its heyday

The quay itself was wooden, because stone walls were hard to build on the shifting mud; wood faggots were used to bind the mud, and then 16-ft-long piles were driven in. Several granite mooring bollards have survived. In the early days vessels of about 100 tons could dock here, with an average water depth of 10ft alongside the main wharf at neap tides, but as time went on the ever-encroaching silt was an increasing problem.

After about 1870 the decline of the Gwennap copper industry spelt trouble for Devoran Quay. In 1876 the County Adit became blocked near its mouth at Twelveheads; the following winter was very wet, and when the pent-up waters in the mines finally broke free so much silt was deposited down-river that from then on ships had to discharge much of their cargo at Point before proceeding to Devoran. The last ship delivered coal at Devoran in 1916.

Restoration work in progress at Devoran Quay

From the far end of the quay you have a fine view of Restronguet Creek, with the woods of the Carclew estate on the right, the engine house of the Carnon Stream Mine on the left, and close at hand in the bed of the creek the remains of embankments. Some of these were created as part of the huge tin-streaming operation (described in a later note) which occupied much of the creek bed from the late 18th century till 1812, when the dam at the seaward end was swept away during a storm; probably others are evidence of attempts by the docks and railway company to divert the Carnon River and its silt away from the wharves.

3 From the end of the quay follow the foreshore to the left, round a small inlet (notice the sleeper blocks scattered about, mainly in the low walls), **and then beside the larger one, Narabo Creek.** This appears to have been the original course of the Carnon River before the quays were built. **Now the path runs beside several ruined buildings - probably warehouses and stables for the railway. Turn right on the gravelled drive, and soon you are back on the road below the Old Quay Inn** - originally called The Commercial, and then until recently the Devoran Inn.

4 Now turn right on to the Old Tram Road, which follows the course of the horse-drawn tramway to Point. Although the rails were taken up in 1919, the tarmac surface was not laid over the granite setts till 1951, and in the intervening decades the track became so rough and muddy as to be almost unwalkable in places. The unspoilt woods and farmland on the opposite side of the creek are parts of the Carclew estate. (See the nore about Carclew in Walk 3.) **After a quarter of a mile or less, the road curves round Tallack's Creek. At the end of this part, just beyond the letter box fixed to a telegraph pole, go down on the right to look at the remains of the engine house of the Carnon Stream Mine.**

THE MINING OF ALLUVIAL TIN IN DEVORAN (RESTRONGUET) CREEK

From the late 18th century until 1812, a big area of the Carnon Valley, from Carnon Gate (where the old main road from Perranwell ran to Truro) to Tallack's Creek, was sealed off by embankments, with a dam at the seaward end: the remains of the dam can still be seen at low water, just to the seaward side of the engine-house wall. Inside this enclosure tin streaming was carried out; ancient tools made of wood and antler were found, plus some gold. In 1812, the dam was swept away during a storm, and now almost the only visible remains of that huge enterprise, which yielded profits of about £5,000, are the low-tide footpaths near the Carclew side and across Tallack's Creek, which follow the lines of embankments. Plenty of tin remained, and by 1818 plans were afoot to sink a shaft in the middle of the creek just below where the tin streaming had ceased, and to erect a powerful steam engine and water pump on the shore. These were complete by 1824. In 1828 the railway company officially complained that the new mine-workings were impeding shipping, and the mine seems to have closed soon after that, but during its short lifetime it made a profit of £28,000. The remaining wall is among the oldest substantial relics of an engine house surviving in Cornwall.

The ruined engine house of Carnon Stream Mine. The logs are being seasoned in preparation for use by Ralph Bird, well known locally for the pilot gigs he builds and restores

Return to the road and continue. The old pump on the right a little later is a reminder that mains water came to the houses near here for the first time only recently; the older ones have their own wells.

5 Nearly half a mile beyond the engine house, immediately past the cottage on the right called The Salt Box, go up the narrow tarmacked lane on the left. At low tide this is the best vantage point for seeing the "Iron Shaft" in the middle of the creek - explained a little later. The lane soon becomes a path. Point Green, at the top, is one of the few genuine "village greens" in Cornwall, and a very pretty one. The right-hand pair of cottages facing you across the green was formerly a pub, the Bell Inn: part of an arch in the middle, now filled in, probably marks the original entrance to the pub. Its name is said to allude to the ringing of a bell to summon the ferryman for a link with Carnon Yard, on the other side of Penpol Creek - an attractive suggestion, but there seems to be no solid evidence for it.

Go down the short flight of steps near the post box, a little way to your right from the place where you came up from the Tram Road. The steps lead down to a small orchard with a well preserved limekiln on the right.

Above: Point limekiln. In the creek can be glimpsed the top of Charles Shaft.

Left: Point Green, from a painting dated 1889. The limekiln, the pub and the smelting works stack are all shown.

Right: Point Green today: the pair of cottages which once formed the Bell Inn. The pump is a fairly recent feature.

The orchard and nearby bungalow, "Gulls Haven", mark the site of a later underwater mining enterprise, the Restronguet Creek Tin Works.

THE RESTRONGUET CREEK TIN WORKS

In 1871 a shaft (Taylor's Shaft) was sunk here to a depth of 108 feet and a cast-iron ventilation shaft (Charles Shaft) was driven down 78 feet to the tin-bearing level in the middle of the creek. Flanged cylinders 6 feet in diameter, 6 feet long and each weighing 2½ tons, cast at the Perran Foundry, were forced into the mud by fastening barges loaded with 250 tons of stone to the top at high tide; when one cylinder was in place, another was fitted to the top and driven down in turn, and so on till the shaft was complete. The top of the "Iron Shaft" can still be seen at low tide. During the next eight years a complex pattern of "levels" was mined between here and the old Carnon Stream Mine, and the workings remained dry even though there was 14 feet of water above them at high tide. A fascinating painting showing the multi-purpose engine house which was built where the orchard now is is in the possession of the Royal Cornwall Museum, Truro. (It is reproduced in the colour section of "Exploring Cornwall's Tramway Trails" Volume 2 and on a larger scale in my late wife's book, "Life by the Fal".) The rotary beam engine pumped from Taylor's Shaft by means of flat-rods, wound to the surface the wagons which also ran along rails in the levels out under the creek, and probably also worked the stamps, of which there were only two heads, since alluvial tin needs little stamping.

This was the last mining venture on (or under) Restronguet Creek, but as recently as the early 1980s an international company, Billiton Minerals, caused much local controversy by putting forward a scheme to dredge the creek bed for the wealth of minerals that still remains. Falling tin prices put paid to that, as to so many earlier and later enterprises.

6 Continuing to the left along the creekside road, you immediately reach what was once known as Daniell's Point, with its long old building, the near end of which is shown as a coal store on the 1908 map. More recently it housed a small shop. During 1990 was converted into two houses.

Point was where the railway line ended, although by 1906 there was an extension towards Penpol to serve the smelting works there; the Daniell family (again see *A History of Truro* Vol. 1) had built a quay here before 1800, capable then of taking ships over 160 tons. The quay, now known as Point Quay, was purchased as a public amenity in 1989 by Feock Parish Council with the aid of £33,000 raised locally through the Point Quay Association. At the same time the orchard opposite "Regatta Cottage" and "Point Quay House" was also bought, and the limekiln there has been brought out of hiding by the voluntary effort of members of the Association and other local people. The name, "Regatta Cottage", alludes to the fact that Point Quay is the setting for the Point and Penpoll Regatta, one of the leading annual events in the local yachting calendar and famous for the excellent teas provided by the local WI.

Opposite the quay is a brick-built pair of houses - a quite unusual sight in these parts. There was a tall stack here, part of the Penpoll smelting works, and when this was demolished the bricks were used to build the houses.

Continue round into Penpol (or Penpoll) Creek. Soon after Black Lane, on the left (perhaps so named because of the smoke from all the industrial chimneys once here), you reach the site of the main smelting works buildings, now occupied by the bungalow called "Polmarion". You may still be able to see relics of the concrete floors or yard, and of flues in the wall behind. On the right here was another wharf, and close to the wall you may be able to make out what could be a small buddle.

SMELTING OF LEAD AND TIN AT PENPOL

In 1817, Sir William Lemon leased land immediately north-east of Point Quay, for the building of a wharf to be named Lemon Quay. By 1827 a lead smelting works had been established beside it. During the next three decades this

The smelting works at Penpol, from a painting made in 1857

expanded northwards along the western shore of Penpol Creek. Long flues were built up to tall stacks on the higher land. By 1880 the works was owned by a London-based company which had converted the buildings for tin smelting. The 1906 OS map indicates that by then work was concentrated on the northern part of the site, that the Redruth & Chasewater line had been extended to serve the smelter, and that storage "hutches" had been built on Lemon Quay. As at Devoran, these were probably at a lower level than the line, so that the contents of the horse-drawn wagons could be simply tipped in. Closure of the smelting works came in 1921.

Go on for another couple of hundred yards, until you come to stepping stones on the right - perhaps submerged. In their place was once a tide mill used to power bone-crushing machinery; beyond it was Bone Mill Pool.

The stepping stones at Penpol. The stream runs through the gap where the waterwheel once stood, and the base of the wall which impounded tidal and stream water is still clear to see (though not shown in this sketch).

7 Now the time for a choice has come: either return directly to Devoran now, or continue to Feock.

For the shorter walk, go to the bridge at the head of Penpol Creek and on past the chapel to a left turning; then follow the directions from point 13 (page 49).

To walk to Feock (and it's very worthwhile), cross the stepping stones

if the water is low enough; if not, walk to the head of the creek and take the track on the right beside the foreshore. Follow track or foreshore round to Penpol Boatyard. (At exceptionally high tides you may have to walk round to the boatyard via the road above, through the Trevallion Park estate.) This part of the foreshore has a heavy scattering of clinker, the most obvious surviving physical evidence of the former smelting works. The boatyard carries out repair work, builds boats from scratch, and places a special emphasis on restoring old timber vessels. During the winter as many as about 60 boats are usually laid up on the hard and foreshore.

Immediately after passing the boatyard take the lane straight ahead (blessed with a wealth of signs: "Private Road", "Public Bridleway" and "Unsuitable for heavy goods vehicles"), **or at low tide continue along the foreshore.** (This is probably the more attractive way, but rough underfoot, and you may have to bestride or duck under a good many mooring ropes and other obstructions, especially at the start.)

8 The foreshore route will bring you to the small headland called Carnon Yard or simply Yard; if you are using the lane, bear right where it forks, after nearly half a mile, to reach the headland.

BOAT-BUILDING AND MINING AT CARNON YARD

This point takes its name from a boat-building yard which appears to have been situated on or very close to the beach. Many locally famous vessels were built here and at Pill Creek (visited later on this walk) by the Ferris family in the earlier part of the 19th century, and even after their yard here was bought by John Stephens in 1858 William "Foreman" Ferris was in charge of the actual boat-building. When Stephens sold the yard in 1880 it was probably taken over by Frank Hitchens, who had already established his own boat-building business in the walled yard, part of which can still be seen, beside the lane leading down to Carnon Yard.

Carnon Yard once had an engine house on it, together with an "Account House" and, no doubt, assorted other mine buildings. They belonged to the Carnon Mine (1835-42). An island was created out in the creek and a shaft twelve feet in diameter was sunk into this. A small pumping-engine was then erected by the shaft. By 1838 212 people were employed, but this was a costly operation, and tin prices fell, so the mine lost about £16,000. The island, known locally as "The Mine Bank", is still visible at low tide and a hazard for yachtspersons when it is submerged, as at least one discovers to his or her cost during most Point & Penpoll Regattas.

From Yard take the lane leading inland. The original Hitchens' boatyard was on the right opposite the old cottage named Carnon Yard. **At the junction, turn right, following the sign to Harcourt** (spelt "Harket" on some old maps, and probably meaning "beside or facing the rock"). **At the bungalow called Tweseldown, go straight on ahead to a narrow path and over the stile.** You will have occasional glimpses of the Pandora Inn across Restronguet Creek to the right: see Walk 3. **After the farm buildings, follow the lane past the houses at Harcourt till you reach the road by a telephone box.**

9 If you want to visit Restronguet Point - about a mile there-and-back - turn right. Otherwise, turn left and take the road to the right just past Porthgwidden gatehouse, into Feock. Porthgwidden is an old house (c. 1830) built by Edmund Turner, one of Truro's MPs. Its estates used to extend as far as Restronguet Point; it is now converted into flats and maisonettes. Polgwynne, further along, has a fine garden running down to the foreshore, occasionally open to the public for charity: to enquire, ring 01872-862612.

10 Soon you come to a right turning signposted Loe Beach, a pleasant spot with a lovely view of Carrick Roads. **Even if you don't want to go right down to the beach (and you may be deterred from doing so by the steep climb back), I suggest you go a short way down this road to join the path to the church,** to take advantage of the view over the beach and out to sea. **The path, which is marked "Feock" by a rather elderly and not very legible sign, is on the left just beyond a wooden garage. At first keep close to the hedge on the left, then continue ahead, eventually passing between a house and the churchyard. Turn right at the road** (look left to see the former school, closed in 1983, when the roll of pupils had fallen to thirteen) **and continue past the lych gate.**

FEOCK

St Feoca's church is said to have been where the last sermon in the Cornish language was preached. The church itself was so heavily "restored" in 1874 that hardly anything old remains, but the detached tower dates from the 13th century. There is also a Norman font and in the south porch a set of stocks. In the churchyard is an old Celtic cross.

Whether there ever was a saint called Feoca is doubtful. The name suggests a female, but if a man perhaps he was the Irish or Scottish Fiacc or Fiacra, said to taken up residence in France as a scholar at the court of Charles the Bald. Alternatively, the village name may derive from the Cornish "feage" or "vegue", "a lofty place". This gains some support from the fact that the upper part of the village is called La Feock, pronounced "La Vaig". The "La" is not French but probably derives from "Lan", "church-site or hermitage".

11 After the right and left bends, take the tarmacked footpath on the right, beside the entrance to the Church Hall car park, which brings you down to Pill Creek.

PILL CREEK

Pill Creek (oddly named, since "pill" means creek) was for a time important to the copper mines as a port for shipping ore and importing coal. Look across the creek from the point where the path brings you down. The right-hand house of the attractive pair was a pub, and the ships docked at the quay below it. The problem with ports like this one and Roundwood Quay, a little further up-river (see Walk 6) was the land communications. (A letter of January 1817 reads, "... such frequent rains for the last month - the roads from the mines to the wharf are so badly cut up, particularly those to Pill, that all the wheel carriages are stopped and the mules are the only conveyance at present.") Canals were considered, but engineers declared them impracticable, and the hills precluded a railway. The arrival of the Redruth & Chasewater Railway at Devoran ensured that Pill Creek would return to peace and quiet.

If the tide is low enough, go down the steps to the foreshore and walk along to the left - but if not, see the note in brackets a few lines below. Near the head of the creek there is a wooden boathouse on the left; go up the tarmacked path just beyond this to return to the road. There turn right, and after a short distance turn sharp left on to a concreted lane, signposted to La Feock. Just past the house called Gelvinack, take the footpath on the right, again signposted to La Feock. (If the tide is too high for walking on the foreshore, return up the same path, turn right at the road, and after about 70m, at the top of the slope, take the footpath on the left, turning left again where signposted to La Feock, just past houses called Seascape and Landfall.) Keep by the hedge on the right - a good view down Carrick Roads from here - **and go through the small gate; now the path curves left and becomes a tarmacked lane before turning right.** After the second house, The Old Grange, notice the pump on the left, and the well at the bottom of a short flight of steps. Mrs S.M.Satchwell, who has written a brief history of the village, *Introducing Feock*, suggests that an unnamed monk may have set up his hermitage beside this well and become known as "the holy man on the hill" or "Saint Feock". (See the note about Feock above.)

12 Turn right at the road, and at the T-junction cross the stile (concrete steps beside a gate) immediately opposite. Walk straight ahead, keeping the hedge to your left. At and just after the next stile you have a good panoramic view of Penpol Creek and beyond to Restronguet Creek and Devoran, with Carn Marth on the skyline. The Carn Brea monument is also visible, just left of the Pennance engine house. **Continue straight on down the field, emerging via a farm gate on to a lane. Cross the stile almost opposite, by Trolver farm,** where two formerly dilapidated old barns have been transformed into impressive-looking houses, and go on in the same direction. **After the next stile you walk among modern bungalows and come to a road. At the road, continue downhill into Penpol, passing the chapel on your right.**

13 Turn left over the bridge. Notice the attractive Bridge Cottage on the left, built in about 1635 "towards the Relife of the poore people". **Walk quite steeply uphill past more old cottages at first, then new houses. Take the first left turning, signed Public Bridleway, and where it joins a tarmacked lane turn right.** This is called The Rope Walk, but no-one seems to know just where the rope walk itself was; perhaps along the side-lane on the left leading to Rope House.

At the road, turn right, then immediately left on to a track, usually muddy. (If it is too muddy, you could instead walk back down the road towards the creek, to rejoin the Tram Road via Point Green.) If you decide to brave the mire, walk along the track behind houses. It dips into a valley at Chycoose Farm and then continues ahead. Still a little more mud to come, but the view of Restronguet Creek a bit further on will compensate. **At the end of the field with a hedge to your left, you could cross the high stile just before a gate and go down to the Tram Road; or go through the gate, keep by the hedge, and turn left down the drive at the next house. Turn right on the creekside road to return to your starting-point.**

At the hairpin bend you may care to turn right, past the Old Quay Inn, and head back along St John's Terrace. Like Belmont Terrace, up to the right, this was built about 1850; both are attractive, but the upper one, slightly less imposing, was presumably built for the railway company's humbler employees. St John's Terrace takes its name from the church, built in 1855-6 and designed by J.L.Pearson, the architect of Truro Cathedral later in his career.

Unless you want to take the bus to Truro or Falmouth, which stops opposite the church, turn left down Market Street, originally named Lemon Street. (See the note about Carclew on page 33.) At the corner as you turn into it is Devoran School, founded in 1846; it recently took over the old Market House, a little way down the street. Now, in 2003, there is talk of the school's moving to a new site elsewhere in the village.

WALK 5

PENELEWEY, PENPOL & COME-TO-GOOD

About two-and-a-half miles.
Can be extended to about eight or ten miles by tacking on the extension to Feock described in Walk 4.

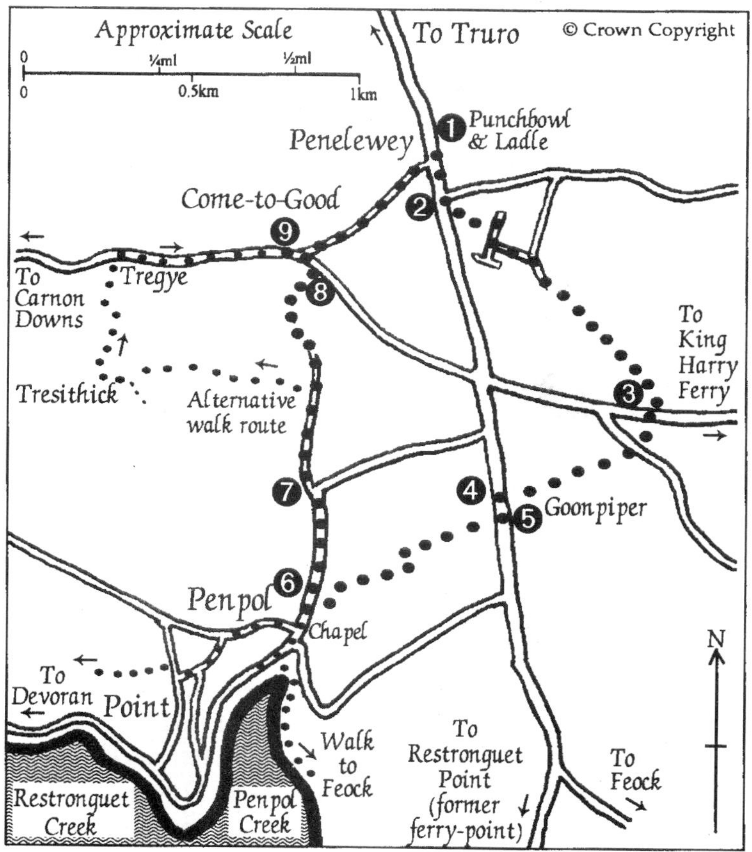

This is a short and easy walk, despite a couple of steepish slopes, passing through attractive countryside, mostly woodland and undulating fields. Here and there you get glimpses of Restronguet Creek and Carrick Roads, and a very short diversion enables you to reach the water (or mud) at Penpol, but the main point of interest on the walk is the famous little Quaker Meeting House at Come-to-Good. The walk starts and ends at or close to a pub, well known in the area for comfort and good food and drink, the Punchbowl & Ladle, usually referred to simply as the Punchbowl. There is nowhere else en route where you could buy provisions or find toilets. The paths are likely to be muddy in places.

To drive to Penelewey, follow the directions for driving to Trelissick at the start of Walk 6. The Punchbowl & Ladle is on the left about three-quarters of a mile beyond the double roundabout. The pub has a car park for customers, but if you don't intend to be one there is a small layby on the left just beyond it. It's for the convenience of those using the public telephone there, but there's room for about three cars without blocking entrances. Another possibility for parking is to take the side-road on the left just past the phone box, where roadside parking should cause no problems so long, again, as you keep well clear of entrances. Truronian bus service 311 (Monday to Saturday) links Truro with the Punchbowl & Ladle: see current timetables.

1 From the pub car park, turn left on the road; walk with care, and keep to the left side, passing the phone box.

2 When you reach the side-road to Cowlands and Coombe on the left, take the signed public footpath which begins at the corner opposite. This narrow little path threads its way among the gardens and houses of a fairly new private estate, known as Wellington Plantation in memory of the woodland that used to occupy this site. Some remnants of it survive, in fact, and we half-filled a bag with sweet chestnuts when we last did this walk. Incidentally, two hundred years ago Truro Races (that is, horse races, and donkeys too!) were usually held on Feock Downs in a field called Waterloo - probably close to here. **At the road turn right, then first left. This brings you to a T-junction with an old thatched cottage opposite; here turn right, following a public footpath sign. Cross what remains of a stile on the right side of a farm gate, then walk diagonally left across the centre of the field and through the gap at the far corner.** (This corner had been churned up by cattle when we were there last, and was the stickiest patch on the walk.) **Still go on in the same direction, making for the right side of a former blacksmith's shop, recently restored. Cross the stile beside it.**

3 Turn right on the road. Again you need to take care, because this is the road to and from the King Harry Ferry, along which drivers tend to hurry. After a few yards, cross the stile on the left, with a footpath sign to Goonpiper. (The name perhaps conjures up some lunatic Scotsman, so it's a bit disappointing to learn that it means merely the downland or unenclosed pasture belonging to the Piper family.) **The path crosses a drive before**

reaching a minor road; cross the stile opposite and continue ahead over two more stiles. After the second of them, keep by the hedge on your right, reaching another stile beside a gate. Notice the view of Carrick Roads to the left here. **Go straight on along a lane open to fields on both sides**: cattle were wandering freely across the lane when we last walked here, so the importance of closing the gate at the end was obvious.

4 Turn left on the road, crossing first to face oncoming vehicles, since this is yet another road which demands careful walking: traffic moves fast on this straight stretch. Luckily you're not on it for long.

5 Turn right at the footpath sign to Penpol, beside Mount Albert Cottage, on to a grassy tractor track running between hedges.

From this high, open ground you get good views, with Carnmenellis hill on the skyline ahead and the big house called Tregye to the right - best seen when you come to a gap in the hedge on that side.

TREGYE

Tregye (say "Tre-guy", as in Fawkes; the name literally means "dog-house") dates from the first decade of the 19th century. For many years the home of various wealthy owners, it became a hotel and restaurant after World War 2. Following the demise of Truro Cathedral School early in the 1980s, Tregye was transformed into the Duchy Grammar School, thanks to the determined efforts and financial support of many of the parents of Cathedral School pupils and members of staff. That, too, is now defunct, and Tregye is now an outpost of Truro College.

Where a gate bars the way ahead, don't go through it, but pause a moment to survey the Penpol valley below; to the left is a glimpse of Restronguet Creek. **The path continues to the left, through another gate, then turns right (there is a yellow waymark arrow) and runs gently downhill between fields, eventually reaching the old house called Millbrook.** (The name is a bit of a mystery, to me at least, since there's no sign of a brook here, or of any other likely power source for a mill. Certainly there was a watermill in the valley not far below, so perhaps the reference is to that - but my late wife, Viv, told me she had been assured, by people who should know, that there was a mill at Millbrook.) **Just past the house there is a stile on the left, but if it is still overgrown carry on down for another few feet before turning left and descending a steep path, with short flights of steps at the top and bottom.**

6 When you reach the road, notice the slight remains of the leat that served Penpol Mill, just below the level of the road on the far side. The mill itself, a corn mill dating from at least the mid-16th century, seems to have been a short way further downstream. A very old photograph of it is reproduced in *Life by the Fal* (page 20). **Turn right on the road to continue the walk ...** But first I recommend a very short diversion to the left for a look at Penpol or Penpoll (Cornish, "head of the pool or creek").

Penpoll Chapel

Up to the left is the chapel, the bank below it a breath-taking mass of primroses in spring.

Bridge Cottage

Beyond the bridge on the right are Penpol Farm and attractive old cottages, the nearest of which, Bridge Cottage, was formerly a house for the poor.

Ahead is Bone Mill Pool, where you may well catch a glimpse of one or two of the egrets that seem to have become semi-permanent residents around the Fal estuary. More in evidence will probably be the swans, although fewer come here now than did at the time the back-cover photograph was taken, when as many as fifty would flock in to be fed by local people concerned for their health following the pollution of these waters by heavy metals in the wake of the closure of Wheal Jane. The drop in numbers had three causes: a good many of the birds, sadly, died; others were taken by RSPCA officials to safer waters; and the remainder congregated to be fed at a spot further up Restronguet Creek, for a reason I'll explain in a moment. Bone Mill Pool is still clearly divided from the rest of Penpol Creek by the remains of the wall built to create a tidal reservoir. The undershot waterwheel which powered the bone-crushing machinery was at the right-hand end of the wall, close to where the stepping stones are now. (See the sketch on page 45.) Not much further away, on the west side of the creek, stood an important smelting works, active until 1921. A lasting legacy of this is the exceptionally high content of lead in the mud near the stepping stones, where the swans were originally fed; hence the decision to move the feeding-place. On the opposite shore is Penpol's only surviving industry (unless you count such things as writing books of walks!), Penpol Boatyard.

The above description scarcely scratches the surface of this interesting place, which has seen changes over the last two centuries more dramatic than almost any other around the Fal estuary. For much more detail read *Life by the Fal* and do Walk 4. (If you have the time and the energy required, you could in fact now add on the extension to Feock, following the directions in the latter part of Walk 4.)

Back to the walk up the wooded Penpol valley now, with the stream down to your left ... Soon you will pass the long gardens of Little Piper and Pipers Barn, which make imaginative use of the stream as a feature.

7 Turn left, following the public footpath sign immediately beyond Pipers Barn. The path is in fact at first a gravelled drive, with the stream still fairly close on the left, though not usually either visible or audible. (A stile on the left is the start of a path to Lower Tresithick and Tregye, a perfectly acceptableand attractive alternative route to Come-to-Good, though it involves more road walking than my recommended one; you may nevertheless wish to try it if you are armed with a suitable map.) Continuing along the drive, you soon have a closer view of Tregye (to the left) than the one mentioned earlier. **Go on ahead through the gate (if it's closed) of Point Clear house, and then through the little gate beside the house. Ignore the side path to the left: continue ahead along this narrow path among trees close to the stream, crossing a rather flimsy stile.** A little scrambling over or around the fallen trunks of trees is involved. **After a few yards along the edge of a field you have to climb over a small wooden gate, with the aid of a few breeze blocks. Soon the woodland section of the path ends, and you go**

diagonally to your right across an open field and pass just to the right of farm buildings. The stile brings you to a road.

8 Turn left on the road, and you will almost immediately reach the Quaker Meeting House at Come-to-Good.

WALK 5
COME-TO-GOOD

Several old Cornish place-names have been anglicised into quaint expressions (Penny-Come-Quick and Readymoney Cove come immediately to mind), but few if any seem so perfectly suited to the place in both their English and their Celtic versions as Come-to-Good ("cwm-ti-coit", valley - house - wood).

The Meeting House, originally a plain rectangular cob-and-thatch building, was built by the Society of Friends in 1710. The gallery or "loft" inside was added in 1717, and several other changes have been made since then, but much of the simple domesticity of the original has survived, and with it an atmosphere that conveys more religious feeling - to me at least - than many a cathedral or temple. The interesting booklet usually on sale inside, whose text is adapted from a talk given by one of the local members, Harry Pallett, explains why the Meeting House should have been built in such an apparently remote spot: in fact this road was once an important route linking Truro with Penryn and Falmouth via the Restronguet ferry. He might perhaps have added that the road is a very direct link between the King Harry Ferry and Chacewater, Redruth and West Cornwall.

David Mudd has an interesting section in his book "Around and About the Fal" on the early history of the Quaker movement in Cornwall, and he states - on what evidence I do not know - that Come-to-Good is "now the oldest Quaker meeting house in England", and "one of only three such thatched, buttressed, clay and straw buildings in the country."

9 From the Meeting House turn left for a few yards, passing a house that usually has a board outside announcing "Antiques", and then take the surfaced drive on the left. After the bungalow it becomes a wide, uphill track lined with oaks. When you are near the top, if you look back you may catch a glimpse of Restronguet Creek. **After passing a few houses you will reach the main road almost opposite the Punchbowl.**

WALK 6

TRELISSICK, COWLANDS, COOMBE & OLD KEA

About eight miles, but two shorter walks are also suggested.

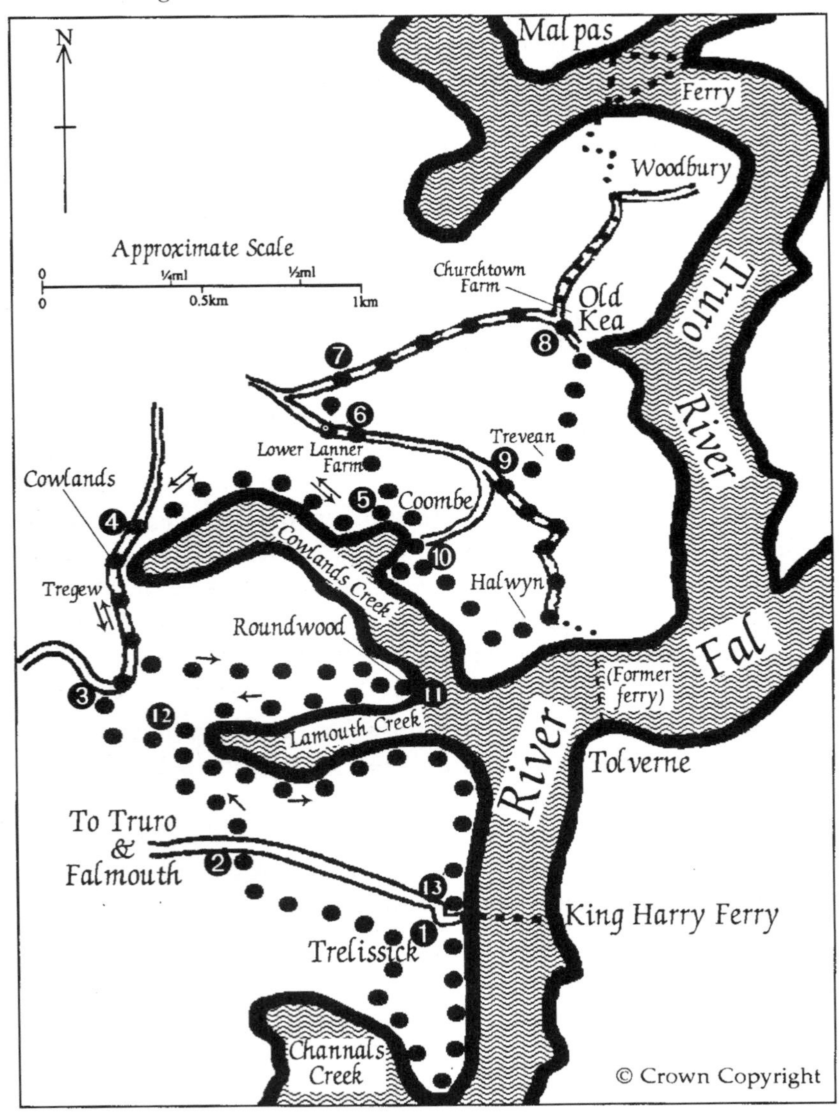

Trelissick makes a good base for a walk, because it provides ample parking (free to National Trust members) and has a shop and restaurant - three things you won't find anywhere else on this route. The walk itself is very beautiful, offering a great variety of open and wooded countryside plus river and creek views, a ruined church, a pretty waterside village, probably some big ships, and a chance to visit the famous garden and the arts-and-crafts gallery at Trelissick. Not much road walking is involved, and most of that is on quiet back roads. The paths are usually muddy in places.

To drive to Trelissick from Truro, take the A39 south towards Falmouth, and at the double roundabout (Playing Place) take the second left turning, just beyond the garage; from there follow the signs to King Harry Ferry. Coming from Falmouth, take the first right turning at the Playing Place roundabout. Trelissick has bus links with Truro, currently Truronian Service 7 Monday - Saturday and First Western National Service 89B on summer Sundays and Bank Holidays. See the Cornwall Public Transport Timetable book for details.

The Water Tower, Trelissick

TRELISSICK

A house was built on this beautiful site about 1750 for a military captain. In 1800 it was bought by R.A.Daniell, nicknamed "Guinea-a-minute" because that was supposed to have been his income from Wheal Towan at Porthtowan, only one of several mines he owned. His son Thomas had the house rebuilt on a grander scale with an Ionic portico, and laid out roads through the estate; only six years later he ran out of cash and sold the property to the Earl of Falmouth. Eventually it came into the hands of the Copeland family of the Spode China Factory at Stoke-on-Trent. In 1955 Mrs Copeland presented the house and 376 acres of parkland to the National Trust, but the house is still lived in by the family and is not open to the public. The garden is open every day between mid-February and early November (from 10.30 am except Sundays, 12.30 pm), and the Woodland Walk is open at all times. Refreshments are available at Trelissick Barn: phone 01872-863486 for details.

1 The route begins with part of the northern section of the National Trust's Woodland Walk; if you haven't already got the NT's leaflet No. 17, available in the shop at Trelissick, I recommend you to buy one. **From the car park at Trelissick, walk away from the house and garden; fork left, go through one of the gates on either side of a cattle grid and follow the road which runs through the park.** (The sketch is of the view to the left as it was when that tree was whole and healthy. In the distance is Pendennis Castle.)

After a second cattle grid, turn right along the path signed Woodland Walk. The modern house among trees to your left is Lis Escop, the Bishop of Truro's residence. **Soon you reach the lodge.**

2 Cross the road (PLEASE BE CAREFUL, because the ferry traffic along this road usually seems to be in a hurry) to the gate opposite, and continue the Woodland Walk. The seat you soon reach is well placed for a pretty view of Lamouth (pronounced "L'mooth") Creek. **The path curves downhill towards the head of the creek.** You will see a small pool down on your left, and a path runs down beside that to a wooden bridge.

<u>For the shortest walk</u>, continue on the upper path as it curves right, picking up the directions in point 12.

<u>For the longer routes</u>, go down the path on the left but not as far as the bridge: turn left again on to the path which runs up the valley, following the course of the stream. After going through the kissing-gate, take the track on the right, over the bridge and up to a road.

3 At the road, turn right, and in less than half a mile you will come to Cowlands ... just four or five houses at the head of a tidal creek. **Continue over the two low bridges.** The second stream evidently once powered a waterwheel here, since the last house is called "Cowlings Mill". (It was "Cownance Mill" on the 1813 OS map; the name derives from the same Cornish words as Kynance: "kew-nans", literally hollow valley, glossed by Oliver Padel as "ravine" - better suited to Kynance than to this gentle landscape!)

4 Now you can walk to Coombe along the foreshore if the tide is out (though one part is always soggy, and here a path runs close to the creekside), or continue a few yards up the road and take the woodland footpath on the right, marked Public Footpath, Coombe. (There is less to see on this route, but it takes you among the orchards for which this area is famous locally .... and you could use the foreshore route later.) **After the house, where the path turns left, bear right over or beside a stile; after a second stile turn right. Now the path runs beside a hedge on the right side of a small field. Continue to the gate at the end, which brings you to a house where bric-a-brac is usually on sale; turn right after the gate and then follow the path to the left by the side of the creek.** You will pass a former Methodist chapel and an old cottage known as "Annie Udy's".

COOMBE

This place is famous locally for its orchards, and in the autumn a very popular Sunday afternoon outing from Truro is to come and buy apples - including some delicious old varieties such as Fairfields - and the small, damson-like Kea plums which are special to this area. At the right season you can pick the plums for yourself from the low-growing trees along Cowlands Creek. A few years back there was a small canning factory at Coombe, just below the first cattle grid on the road up from the creek, where William Gunn & Co. packed Coombe Black Plums in heavy syrup into cans indicating, in a manner unlikely to satisfy modern EEC requirements, "Nett weight of contents about 2½lbs." For over a century until about 1980, other members of the Gunn family were behind another local business, that of "rinding", stripping by hand oak bark for use in the curing of fishing nets and hides. Most of the bark was used at Croggon's tannery, Grampound, about which details are given in Walk 18 of "From the Roseland to St Austell Bay". The tannery was still active until 2000, but the rinding came to an end much longer ago because too few suitable trees were available. (A sketch of Coombe is on page 6.)

5 When you reach the head of Coombe Creek, where most of the houses are, you could again shorten the walk by returning to Trelissick now, following the directions from the start of point 10 (page 68).

But for the full walk, take the footpath on the left, signposted Lower Lanner Farm. Where the main path curves left towards Cowlands, go straight on up and over the stile. Follow the direction indicated by the yellow arrow, slightly to the right of the highest part of the ridge in front

of you, then go through the small gate bearing another arrow. This arrow again points half-right, but in fact the path heads slightly left from the gate, through an open gateway and along the left side of the next field. From up here you get good views of Cowlands and Coombe Creeks behind, the lonely tower of Old Kea church to the right, and Malpas further off. **Another gate brings you to a road.**

6 Turn left, and after a few yards, when you reach Lower Lanner Farm, go through the gate on the right (that is, on the opposite side of the road); here a short path along by the hedge brings you to a stile and another road. From the path there are again good views, including perhaps glimpses of the top of the small spire of St Michael Penkevil Church, and Tregothnan, the seat of Lord and Lady Falmouth, among trees on the far side of the river.

7 Turn right, and continue for about half a mile to Old Kea, where a few years ago you would probably have been greeted by a herd of goats. The goats have gone now. The old sign announcing "Goats Crossing" was repainted to read "Mud on Road"; the sign has gone now, but not the mud.

The remains of the church are worth a visit.

OLD KEA

Kea, otherwise Che or Kee, appears to have been a monk from Glastonbury who founded a monastery here during the 5th century before going on to settle in Brittany, but you may prefer the more picturesque stories telling how he floated across from Ireland in a granite trough, and how in later years he attempted to make peace between King Arthur and Modred. A new parish church of St Kea was built on the western side of the A39 in 1802 when the original one, very distant from most of the houses in the parish, fell into disrepair; the font, pulpit, three bells and several other features of the old church were taken to the new one. (So, too, some fifty years later, was a pig trough from a nearby farm, claimed to be the very vessel in which St Kea had made his voyage.) Now all that remains here is the strangely impressive 15th-century tower, the victim of at least one lightning strike and slowly disintegrating; it is said to have been spared from demolition because it is a picturesque detail in the view from Tregothnan. This tranquil place, well known for its jackdaws, is especially lovely in early spring when in some years the churchyard is a mass of snowdrops. The small mission church near the tower is worth a visit. It was built in 1853 and enlarged ten years later. The ancient cross-shaft that stands near the entrance was found beneath the old church when that was demolished, and is likely to be a relic of St Kea's monastery. (Incidentally, the 1802 church, renowned for its ugliness and badly built, was itself replaced in 1894-5.)

A recommended diversion if you have time and energy to spare, because it's almost a mile there-and-back, is to go down the lane leading to Woodbury Farm (turning left at Churchtown Farm as you arrived at Old Kea). Just before you reach the gate at Woodbury there is a footpath left, down through woodland to the banks of the Truro River opposite Malpas - an unusual view of this attractive village. There is a ferry connection between here, Malpas and the promontory opposite, where the ferryman's cottage is, but it can operate to and from Woodbury only within an hour or so of high tide. **Return to Old Kea by the same route.**

Old Kea church tower as seen from the path you walk along next

8 Go on down the lane past the church, with Church (or Churchtown) Creek to your left, and continue ahead along the signed footpath, which after a few yards runs between electric fences. After the farm gate turn right and follow the track past the farm buildings to the road. From the track if conditions are clear and the foliage is not too thick you will be able to see Truro School and the Cathedral in the distance, but a better view of Truro comes a little later.

9 Turn left for Halwyn, then keep left at a farm entrance (Higher Trelease). Notice the view of Truro from here, from the farm gate on your right at the corner. The road now becomes a rough track, once no doubt a packhorse lane serving the ferry connection with Tolverne.

When you come to the sign directing you right for Coombe, another recommended diversion is to bear left and continue down the lane - not an official footpath, but usually open to walkers. Ignore the side track on the right at a wooden farm gate. Go through the metal farm gate ahead, beyond which the lane dwindles to a path. This soon brings you down to the foreshore opposite Tolverne.

TOLVERNE

Tolverne Manor, on high ground about half a mile east of the river, belonged to the Le Sor family until through marriage it became one of the many seats of the Arundells early in the 15th century. (See the notes on Lanherne and Trerice in "Around Newquay".) Laurence O'Toole in his book on the Roseland traces the "notable decline" in the Tolverne branch of the family: "The last of the line died at the end of the eighteenth century, a pauper living on the parish." Henry VIII is said to have stayed at Tolverne for two nights when he was visiting his newly-built castles of Pendennis and St Mawes, though, as O'Toole points out, there is no firm evidence that Henry ever set foot in Cornwall. The name, Tolverne, probably means something like "hill brow" (from the Cornish, "tal bron").

"Smugglers Cottage", reputedly at least 500 years old, is now a favourite stopping place for pleasure boats plying the Fal. It has been the home of the Newman family since 1934. Originally there were two cottages, one of which was an alehouse and the other a one-up, one-down thatched cottage for the ferryman - or ferrywoman, since there is a tradition that at one time the ferry was operated by a lady known as Bessie who was accused of witchcraft. The association of this neighbourhood with smuggling is confirmed by Thomas Cragoe in his guide to the Fal (1876): he writes of a "sanguinary conflict" between smugglers and excisemen that took place near the cottage in about 1800. He also mentions the granite "sinking stones" which were used by smugglers to anchor kegs of contraband liquor to the river bed below the lowest water-mark till the danger of detection was past. "Some of these stones," he adds, "are still kicking about the old farm places bordering the river" ... but that was a long time ago.

This is an area with many World War 2 associations: there are relics of

Lamouth Creek

Walk along the other side of the creek, round to King Harry Reach.

KING HARRY REACH

The "King Harry", identified in some old guide books as Henry VIII, is now generally thought to have been Henry VI: the Arundells of Tolverne demonstrated their loyalty to the House of Lancaster during the Wars of the Roses by dedicating a chapel to Our Lady and King Henry on the Roseland side. Little if anything of it remains. Otherwise known as King Harry Passage, this quite narrow channel is remarkable for the depth of water: about 50 feet for much of its width and 80 feet in places. Since it is one of the cheapest places in the country to lay up ships that are temporarily redundant, or queuing for a berth at Falmouth Docks, or awaiting their last voyage to the scrapyard, there are sometimes dozens here, manned by skeleton crews. The one-time educational cruise ship, SS Uganda, later employed as a hospital ship during the Falklands war, had her last British home here for a few sad months before she went to the Far East to be broken up.

13 The road you eventually descend to leads to the King Harry Ferry.

WALK 6
KING HARRY FERRY

In 1988 the King Harry Steam Ferry Company published an interesting booklet in celebration of its centenary. The present ferry, built at Penryn in 1974, is powered by diesel engines, but it still operates by means of chains fixed to either bank. Before the advent of steam power in 1888, horses, as well as people and their carriages, were precariously ferried across in a flimsy rowing boat.

The drawing reproduced here, taken from Thomas Cragoe's little guide (1876), gives a fair impression of it. According to the King Harry booklet, "It was usual for a man to be posted at Turnaware Point, to retrieve boat and tide-swept animals!" Laurence O'Toole, in "Place and the Sprys", quotes a 19th-century account of the ferry: "When they (bullocks) arrived at the ferry you drove them into a cattle house by the water's edge where they were roped together. At one time they would be hitched to the back of the boat and driven into the water. They had to swim for it. That was in the days of the rowing ferry. Some job it was with two men rowing. Everyone had to give a hand on the oars." Peter Gilson's "The Upper Fal" traces the history and development of the ferry in a sequence of about a dozen photographs supported by detailed commentary.

You can return directly to Trelissick by turning right, walking up the hill and eventually entering the grounds via the door beside the water tower; but the road is a rather boring uphill trudge and often busy with ferry traffic, so I recommend you to continue the Woodland Walk (up steps beside Bosanko's Cottage, opposite the point where you came down to the road). After rather more than half a mile of very attractive walking, with glimpses of the water between the trees that were probably planted to provide shelter for the gardens at Trelissick, this brings you round

into Channals or Channels Creek, where there is a small beach. Shortly before reaching that you have a good view of Thomas Daniell's Ionic portico fronting Trelissick House.

Conclude the walk by going up the hill above the beach, passing to the left of the house. Towards the top of the slope, it's worth pausing to look back at the fine view along Carrick Roads to Pendennis and the open sea, as illustrated by my sketch on page 60.

A cross-Channel ferry laid up in King Harry Reach, as seen from the Woodland Walk, March 1989

WALK 7

RUAN LANIHORNE & LAMORRAN

About six miles.

A shorter route and an extension of about one mile are described.
Walks 7 and 8 could be linked. The map is at the start of Walk 8 (page 77).

Since the early years of the 19th century, though not today, the upper reaches of the Fal have been used to carry away china clay waste, and thousands of tons must have been deposited at the point where the river met tidal water. ("The ugly white river of Fal discharges its burden of sand and gravel into the pretty arm of Falmouth Haven, called Ruan River" - so wrote Charles Henderson in 1928.) This walk starts by crossing the salt marsh created largely by that process. (I have been told that an attempt to stream for tin was made at Foxhole Creek, between Lamorran and Sett Bridge, and the streamers found that the depth of the china clay deposit there was 49 feet. Hamilton Jenkin in *Mines and Miners of Cornwall*, Part XIII, quotes an advertisement in the Mining Journal of 9 December 1843 offering for sale "Tin Work Bounds from a little above Ruan Lanihorne as far down the River as Lamorran Point" - a reminder that the waste products of tin streaming over the centuries have also contributed to the silt.)

Much of the route is within the vast Tregothnan estate owned by Lord Falmouth; it passes through beautiful woods, open farmland, and then more woods beside a creek where the tiny church of Lamorran nestles among a few pretty houses. The walk is based on Ruan Lanihorne, one of the most attractive and interesting villages around the Fal. The main walk is almost entirely on quiet roads and well-made tracks. A worthwhile short extra is suggested, in the form of a woodland path inland beside the Fal. The only pub on the route is in Ruan, and there is no shop. Telephone boxes are available at Ruan and Lamorran.

To drive to Ruan Lanihorne from Truro, take the A39 eastwards. About a mile past Tresillian, turn right for Tregony, and as soon as you have crossed the bridge over the Fal there, turn right, signposted Ruan Lanihorne. This road runs beside the Fal. From Falmouth the best route is via the King Harry Ferry. After the crossing, drive via Philleigh to Ruan High Lanes, taking the minor road left to Ruan Lanihorne from there. There is (2002) no convenient bus service for this walk.

The King's Head is an attractive pub (rebuilt after the old thatched inn was burnt down in 1898), and a deservedly popular eating place. (Which king, by the way: Henry VIII or Charles I?) If you intend to be a customer, you could

WALK 8

RUAN LANIHORNE, TRELONK, TRENESTRALL & TREWORGA

About four miles, with a possible extension of almost a mile. Directions are also given for a shorter walk, about three miles. Walks 7 and 8 could be linked.

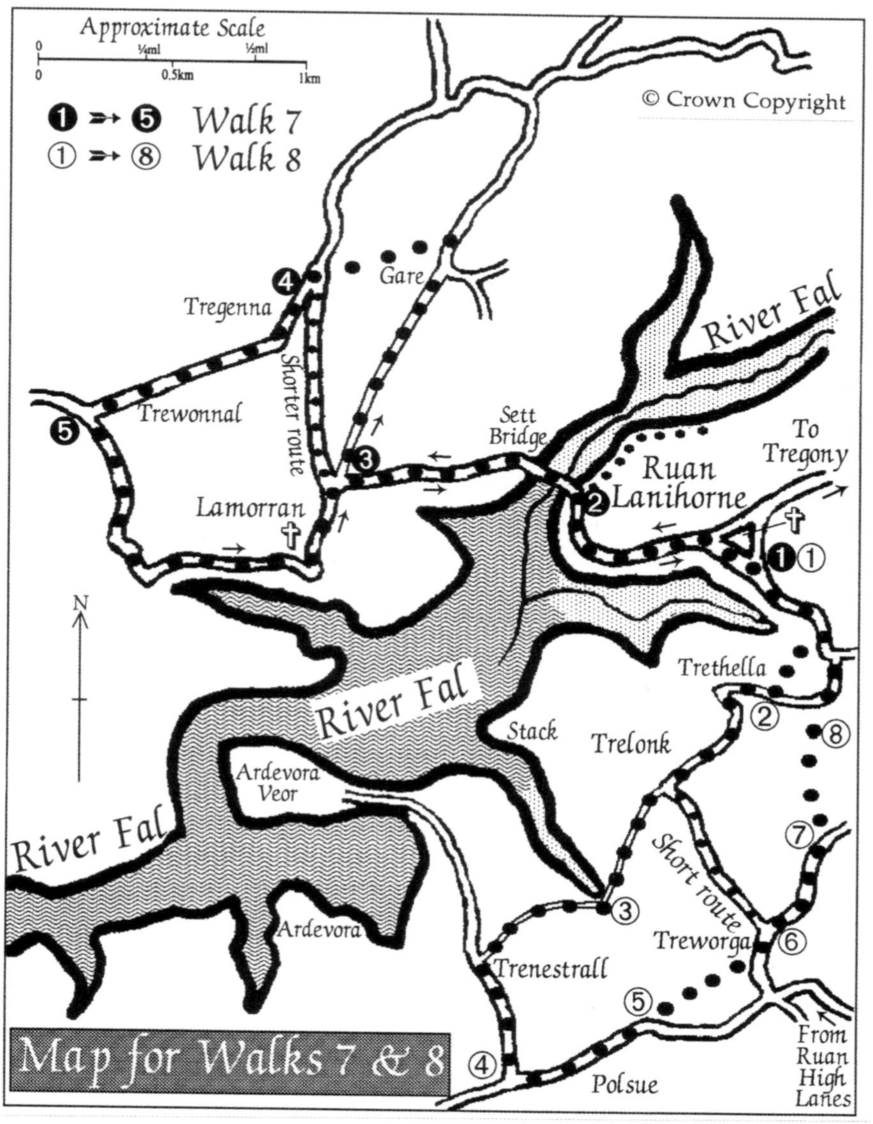

WALK 8

This is a gentle, easy walk through very remote-feeling countryside with occasional glimpses of the river. There are few trees, in great contrast to the other recommended walk from Ruan Lanihorne. The suggested extension to the start of the private road down to Ardevora Veor should not be missed, because the view from this remote spot is exceptional, even by the usual standards of the Fal area. Most of the route is on minor roads or well-made tracks, but there are some paths across fields which are likely to be wet and muddy in normal Cornish weather. At one point near the end of the walk there is a small stream to cross without the assistance of a bridge, and you might be glad of wellies there. There is no shop on this walk, and the only pub is at Ruan Lanihorne. Treworga has a phone box.

For directions to Ruan Lanihorne and comments on parking, see Walk 7. If you are dependent on buses, you could make use of Western National services 51/51A/51C (2000-2001 details), which link Truro and St Mawes with Ruan High Lanes. From there it's about half a mile to Treworga: take the road towards Philleigh and the King Harry Ferry, and then the first right turning, as shown on the sketch map. This will bring you to point 6 in the directions, near Treworga.

1 From the church, walk past the King's Head. Soon you reach Ruan Mill, where the former position of the waterwheel can easily be deduced from the course of the old leat. Notice the bell on the top of the white house a short way beyond: this was once the village school. **Opposite "Tregellas", take the path signposted on the left side of an old building** which was till quite recently a blacksmith's shop: when I was last there, in September 2002, there was still a horseshoe on the door, but the building was being converted into a holiday let, and the builder didn't expect the horseshoe to survive. **The right of way goes straight up the field: make for the slight dip on the skyline** - and don't miss the lovely view behind, up a valley. (The extent to which the landscape has changed over the centuries is shown by the fact that seashells have been dug up in this valley.) **At the top of the slope, go through the two wooden gates and walk almost straight on - just a little to the right - and through a kissing-gate. Go right ahead for a few yards and then down the flight of steps on your left.**

2 Turn right on the road - not up the drives sharp-right. After less than 100 yards, a footpath on the left cuts off a corner. The path is quite attractive (through woodland, over a footbridge and stile, then up to the road, where you turn left); but it's sometimes rather soggy and/or

overgrown with brambles and nettles, so you may prefer to continue up the road, which bends sharply left. Continue uphill past the new-looking (in 2002) entrance and drive to Trelonk and the later group of cottages and farm buildings at the older entrance.

TRELONK

Whitaker's "History of Ruan Lanihorne" mentions a tradition that "there was a city at Trelonk formerly, and that a King resided in it." The city stretched as far as Reskivers, near Tregony. There is at least a grain of truth in this, because in the middle ages there was a village called Sheepstall or Sheepstors at the place now called Porters, very near Reskivers. (See the note on Ruan Lanihorne in Walk 7.) Whitaker believed that Trelonk meant "Long House", and for him this confirmed that it was originally the seat of a Baron; modern Cornish studies, however, explain the name as "farm by the gorge or gully".

Over the brow of the hill, close to the water, is the tall, square, elegant stack of what was once Trelonk Brickworks, active from 1891 to 1907. (It can't be seen at this point in the walk, but you get a few glimpses of it later, as well as from near Sett Bridge on Walk 7.)

otograph by Barbara Tripp

To maintain access to the quay at Ruan, the silt, rich in china-clay waste, was constantly dredged, and some of it was baked in kilns at Trelonk to make the bricks of which many nearby farms (and, it was recently found, some of the more recent parts of St Mawes Castle) are built. Liz Luck mentions that "a tramway used to run out from the quay to the river channel so that loading could be carried out at all stages of the tide"; Jeanette Ratcliffe (Cornwall Archaeological Unit) thinks it likely that a long pipe, part of which is still visible below high-water mark, extended from the foreshore to suck up silt, and that this pipe may have been misinterpreted as the remains of a tramway.

Ruins of buildings on the opposite side of Tuckingmill Creek appear to be those of a clay dry associated with the brickworks. Two photographs of the brickworks in use are in Peter Gilson's "The Upper Fal".

A hide for birdwatching at Trelonk has been constructed by the RSPB and the Cornwall Birdwatching and Preservation Society; a key is available to Society members. For details, write to Mr G. Jackson, Curgurrell Corner, Curgurrell, Portscatho, Truro. For details of the nature reserves here and at Ardevora, contact the Cornwall Wildlife Trust's Warden, Mr S. Gay, Portscatho (01872-580518).

For the shorter walk, continue on the road as it bends left after Trelonk farm. This takes you to Treworga, where you turn left and follow the directions from point 6.

For the full walk, go straight on down the rough track; it's clear at first, but later becomes rather overgrown, and you may have to walk along the field edge beside it. Eventually you will reach a footbridge at the marshy head of Tuckingmill Creek. The name refers to the process of "fulling", that is, cleaning new woollen cloth of grease by scouring and beating. Fuller's earth was used to help absorb the grease. An interesting account of the processes involved is included by Geoffrey Grigson in his classic book about Pelynt, *Freedom of the Parish*: see *Around Looe, Polperro & Liskeard.*

3 Follow the track round to the right. A "green lane", sunk deep between hedges for much of its length, it is obviously old. Was it once, perhaps, a pack-horse trail serving the long-gone tucking mill? **It will bring you to Trenestrall Farm; turn left at the road there if you don't want to include the short diversion described next.**

But I strongly recommend you to turn right for the diversion, to the viewpoint above Ardevora. After less than half a mile of narrow road with high banks (from which at one point you get a good view ahead of the brick-works stack at Trelonk) you suddenly emerge at open fields with a truly memorable panoramic view including Ardevora and Ardevora Veor farms,

Lamorran on the far side of the river, and the top of the Trelonk stack further right. Please do not trespass by walking beyond the "Private" sign beside the cattle-grid. **Return the same way.**

ARDEVORA AND ARDEVORA VEOR

A beautiful and remote spot, famous for its birdlife, which includes overwintering spotted redshanks, plus ring plovers and the occasional osprey, spoonbill and avocet. More common are black tailed godwits, golden plovers, dunlin, teal and shelduck, the last of which sometimes nest in rabbit burrows. (The name Ardevora, pronounced with the stress on the second syllable, means "beside the waters".... Compare Devoran, "waters" - a place where three streams meet the tidal waters. Veor means "great".)

During the early 1830s schemes were proposed to link Ardevora Veor with the china-clay district. At first a canal was suggested, but this was abandoned in favour of a mineral railway, to be called the Cornwall Central Railroad. It was finally decided, however, that the ideal port for the china-clay industry was Par. (Compare the note on St Just, Walk 10.) Laurence O'Toole in "The Roseland" writes of a scheme hatched by a local squire, John Penhallow Peters, who had built his own lime kilns at Ardevora, to construct a railway from Philleigh parish to St Stephen-in-Brannel, "for cheap conveyance of lime, manure etc., to improve agriculture in the Roseland ... to supply iron, coal and groceries cheaply ..." This scheme was also devised in the 1830s, and also came to nothing; whether in fact the two schemes were actually one and the same I do not know.

At Trenestrall (or Trenestral) you pass various interesting farm buildings and houses, and finally you reach what counts in this remote-feeling area as a main road.

4 Turn left. Soon you pass the drive to Polsue Manor, which has been a hotel or guest house since 1934; then the road descends into a valley.

5 At the lowest point, just after crossing the stream (though you may not

notice it), take the footpath on the left at the point where the road curves right. (In 1989 there was a footpath sign at the gap in the hedge, but by 1995 only the post which used to carry the sign was still in place, and that was still true seven years later.) **You now enter a field which whenever I have walked here was planted; the footpath had been ploughed up and not reinstated. (If the field is too muddy for comfortable walking, you could keep to the road instead and take the first left turning, rejoining the suggested route at point 6.) The right of way goes up the field towards the right, gradually diverging from the field-edge alongside the road.** A view of Tuckingmill Creek, the Fal and the brickworks stack opens up to the left. **When you are high enough to see farm buildings ahead, go about 50m. to the right of them, where there is a gap giving access to the road. Turn left on the road.**

5 Continue along the road through the attractive hamlet of Treworga, ignoring the left turning by the phone box. ("Treworga" seems to mean "farm with the low or broken-down hedge".) Notice the pump on the right. Climbing roses were in full bloom at Treworga Farmhouse when my wife and I were there on 23rd April. **Next comes a very pretty stretch, down into another valley.**

6 At the bottom, after two driveways on the left, the road bends right; here you cross a stone stile on the left, beside a footpath sign to Ruan Lanihorne. Now walk just to the right of straight ahead and cross a tiny stream (no more really than a boggy patch in summer) to another stile. Continue in the same line to the next stile, then walk with the hedge on your right; after the gap, it's on your left. Go through the gateway (yellow waymark arrows on a wooden post) and still continue straight ahead, cutting off the field corner to join the track where it bends left. (One of the arrows at the gateway seems to indicate keeping to the field edge all the way, and indeed this may be easier if the field is planted, but the official right of way is as I have just described.)

7 After the gateway (where there is now - September 2002 - no gate, despite a request to close it behind you!), **ignore the farm track on the right, but turn right on the surfaced road. At the T-junction turn left, and this brings you back to Ruan. The best way to finish the walk, I think, is to take the left fork down to the lower road near the little Ruan River, where many of the older and most attractive buildings are.**

Not unexpectedly, the name of one of the houses indicates that there was once a limekiln along here. Ken Isham's book, *Lime Kilns and Lime Burners in Cornwall* (Cornish Hillside Publications, 2000), has an interesting photo dated c.1890, showing the kiln, built early in the 19th century; it was working till about 1920, and stood to its full height till about 1955. Nothing of it remains now, says Mr Isham, so presumably what looks like a kiln in the house's garden is a modern reconstruction. At least one earlier kiln preceded that one: it is known to have been working by 1733. Some of the other buildings look as if they originated as warehouses serving the now-vanished quay on the left side, which also shows in the photo mentioned above; and one pair of cottages take their names from the castle which once stood close by. (See the note on Ruan Lanihorne in Walk 7.)

Before long, a narrow lane on the right takes you up beside the church to your starting point.

WALK 9

ST JUST, MESSACK AND TURNAWARE

St Just church / Messack Point round walk: nearly 4 miles
Extension to Turnaware: about 2 miles

The National Trust bought Messack Farm in 1999 and proceeded to create new footpaths around the Messack peninsula, through undulating fields and woodland with wonderful views of St Just Creek, Carrick Roads and beyond. This is as fine a walk as any around the Fal, and all the more so if you extend it by visiting Turnaware, another spectacular viewpoint and a place of special appeal to those with an interest in recent history, because the evidence that it was one of the D-Day embarkation points is clear to see.

There is nowhere en route where you can buy food, but if the weather is favourable for picnicking there are several ideal spots for it along the way.

The recommended start / end point for the Messack walk or the full route including both Messack and Turnaware is the car park at St Just church; directions to that are given in the introduction to Walk 10. For Turnaware only, you may be able to park at the southern end of the private road leading to Commerrance Farm and Turnaware Point, where this meets the minor road near Carwarthen (grid reference SW 846 370; points 7 and 10 on the sketch map and in the directions). This latter parking place would also give you more flexibility: for example, you could do the round walk to Messack Point without including St Just, thus reducing the distance by more than a mile. During the season, however, you may be unable to find space there: there is room for only a few cars.

1 Having left your car in the St Just church car park, return to the road, then turn right and immediately right again along a wide drive. When you reach the turning circle take the path on the right, following the sign St Just Holy Well. After a small stile (where the well, whose water is used for baptisms, is on your right), turn left, and at the foot of this short path turn right along the public footpath, which now for a little over half a mile runs quite close to the waters (or mud, depending on the state of the tide) of St Just Creek. The deeper water, where the creek opens out into Carrick Roads, is known as St Just Pool.

ST JUST POOL

I hope it won't spoil the tranquil beauty for you to learn that for many years St Just Pool acted as the quarantine station for Falmouth Harbour, where any

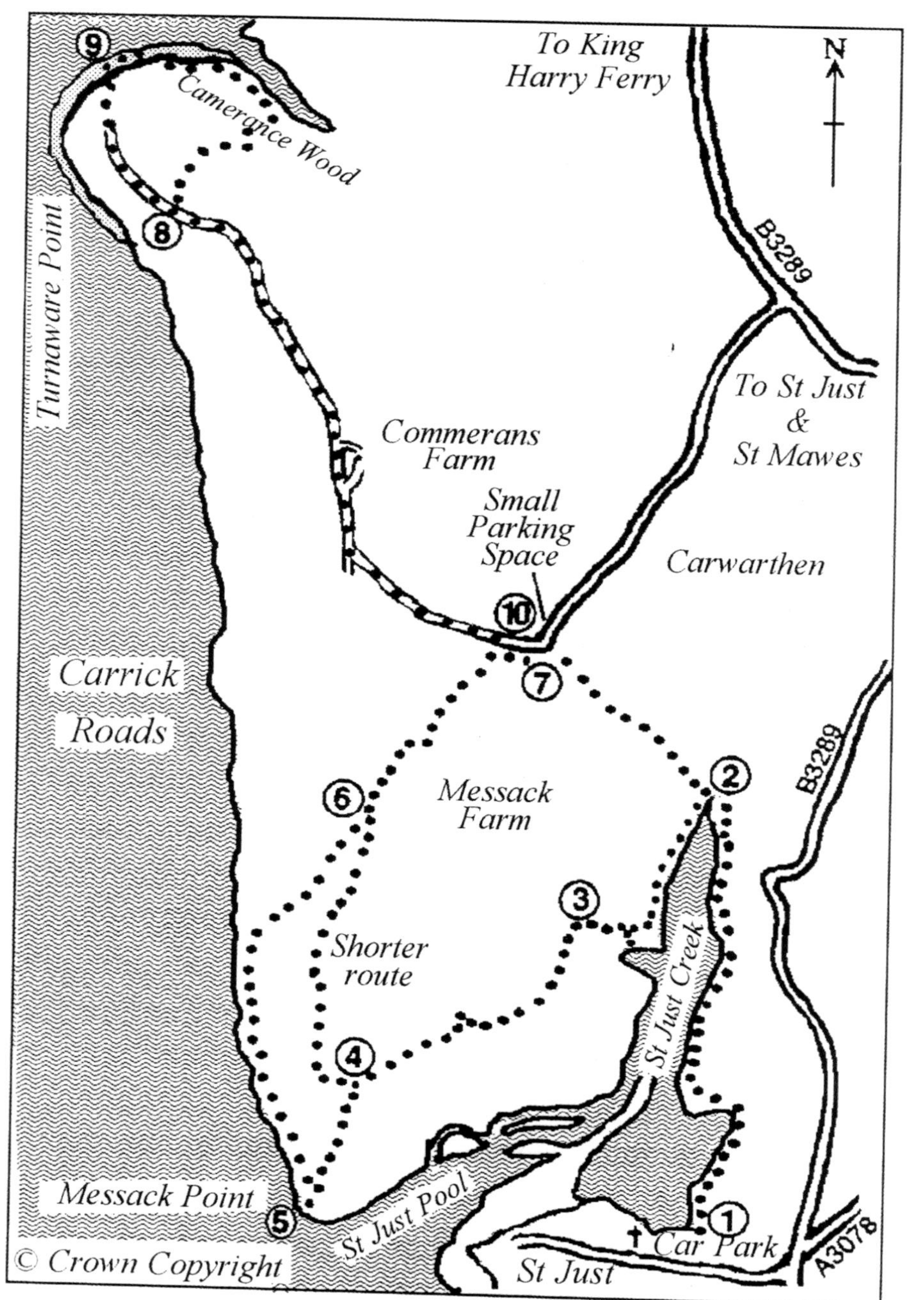
To King
Harry Ferry
N
B3289
Camerance Wood
Turnaware Point
9
8
To St Just
&
St Mawes
Commerans
Farm
Small
Parking
Space
Carwarthen
10
7
Carrick
Roads
2
B3289
6
Messack
Farm
3
Shorter
route
St Just Creek
4
Messack Point
5
St Just Pool
1
Car Park
A3078
St Just
© Crown Copyright

ship suspected of carrying infectious disease would have to wait until cleared. The tranquillity was certainly shattered by the spectacular end of a ship being fumigated here in 1820, as described by Peter Gilson in "The Lower Fal".

St Just could have been a very different place if plans seriously considered by 19th and early 20th century industrialists had come to fruition. In about 1871 the Cornwall Mineral Railways Company had proposed building a line from Kernick Mill near Trethosa (north of St Stephen-in-Brannel) to St Just Pool for the transportation of china clay and iron ore. The slump of the mid-1870s killed that scheme, but a variation of it was put forward shortly before World War 1, and the St Just Ocean Wharves and Railways Bill was passed by a Lords committee in 1919. This time it was opposition within the docks, railway and china-clay industries that put paid to it - and St Just remained a rural idyll. (Compare the note on Ardevora Veor in Walk 8.) (Details from "A History of the Cornish China-Clay Industry" by R.M.Barton.) Laurence O'Toole in "The Roseland" mentions what I presume to have been yet another scheme, proposed "a few decades ago" (he was writing in the late 1970s), to turn St Just into a commercial port; he adds, "The lack of a railway, and the additional expense of building new roads stopped the scheme."

After the first few yards, look back for the very pretty view of the church. There's plenty more to attract the eye, of course, including the lush-looking gardens of two houses. **Beyond a wooden stile, a waymark arrow on a garage wall beside the second house directs you left, up past a log-store, to a second wooden stile.** Below to the left now you see the boatyard on St Just Bar. **After a kissing gate, the path continues along the bottom edge of a large field, eventually bringing you to the woodland at the head of the creek, where there is a second kissing gate followed by a concrete footbridge and a stile at the point where you enter the National Trust's Messack Farm property.**

2 Here turn left, following the sign, Messack Point. The path keeps fairly close to the bottom edge of the creekside field at first, and a wooden gate takes you through the first field boundary hedge. Soon after that you will find three wooden gates in quick succession on the left. The first gives access to a small field with a fine view across the creek to the church; below is a little rocky beach, and from the second gate you can get down to that. This tiny inlet, known as The Poth (from the Cornish *porth*, cove or harbour), with its picturesquely gnarled and seaweed-festooned old treestumps, makes an ideal picnic spot.

St Just Creek from The Poth

3 Turn left through the third gate. After crossing the little stream by a plank bridge, and a deep-cut drainage channel by an impressive structure combining staircase, bridge and gate, the path goes uphill, through a gap in the sturdy stone hedge on the right soon followed by another wooden gate, then keeps close to the hedge on your left. The path crosses a tarmacked drive which leads to Messack House (kissing gates on either side), and now, as you walk beside the wire fences protecting a row of recently-planted saplings in their plastic tubes, the view to the left takes in most of St Just Creek and reaches to Pendennis Castle.

4 Immediately beyond the next gate, you will find: a seat to admire the splendid view of Carrick Roads and/or to eat your picnic; a plaque recording the National Trust's acquisition of Messack Farm; and a clearly signposted choice of ways. The shorter route, which is easy to follow without the need for directions, keeps to high ground and provides more panoramic views; if you go that way, pick up the directions for the longer walk at point 6. But I strongly recommend the alternative, which is actually not very much longer, and is far more interesting and attractive.

Having passed through the gate, then, follow the sign to Messack Point. The path, which is not very clearly defined, runs ever-more-steeply downhill: head for the gate nearer to the right-hand group of Monterey

Approaching Messack Point

pines. This admits you to a short path down to the rocky foreshore at the Point. Here you have the ideal viewpoint from which to survey the long western shoreline of Carrick Roads and Falmouth Harbour, and to watch the seabirds and the maritime activity - endlessly fascinating, especially in summer, when you have yachts, speedboats with or without water ski-ers, sailboarders and River Fal pleasure boats (complete with interesting commentary, sometimes audible on shore) along with the occasional oyster fisher or crabber and the commercial vessels, perhaps waiting for berths at Falmouth Docks. It's another excellent picnic spot, provided you have something soft to sit on!

MESSACK POINT

The name possibly derives from an old Cornish word meaning "open fields, open country", apt enough for the farmland above. On the foreshore, a few yards to the left of where the path brings you down, is an old granite pillar which marks the eastern end of the dividing line between Falmouth and Truro Harbours. The western end is at Penarrow Point, just south of Mylor Creek: see Walk 2, point 8.

5 To continue, take the obvious path on the right, following the shoreline north - in my opinion one of the loveliest walks anywhere around the Fal, enhanced as it is by the generous planting of young trees which complement the older woodland. One short section, where a small stream runs below the path, is usually sticky even in a dry summer, but we enjoyed using the seat there - a chance to study the lush vegetation and watch the many butterflies, such as the comma sunning itself on a twig when we were there. Beyond that point the path climbs steadily beside the deep stream-bed, and soon leaves the valley via a wooden gate.

6 The path continues ahead (slightly right if you have come here by the shorter route), with the hedge on your right at first, but at the end of the first field you go through a couple of gates, after which the hedge is on your left. On the skyline to the right now, the spire is that of Gerrans church. **Beyond another gate, the path bends to the right, soon reaching a minor road via one last gate.**

7 To return to St Just church, go through the kissing gate on the right and pick up the directions at point 10.

To continue to Turnaware Point, turn left, along the concrete drive to Commerrans Farm, which, though marked "Private Road", is open to visitors to the National Trust property at Turnaware. Soon again panoramic views open up: straight ahead at one point early on you can see the hill called Carn Marth, with the engine house of Pennance Mine on the left-hand slope; further left are Four Lanes hill and Carnmenellis, both with tall masts. The views of Carrick Roads and beyond are at their most extensive after you have passed the farm buildings.

8 A kissing gate admits you to the National Trust property. Here you could continue along the main road to the Point, but I recommend that instead you turn right and go through the other kissing gate. The path beyond that heads uphill across a field to a third kissing gate on the edge of Camerance Wood - a delightful spot at any time of year, but especially in bluebell time (May/June). (The name derives from the Cornish, *cam*, crooked, curved, plus *gweras*, ground.) **Following the main path round to the right eventually brings you to steps downhill. The path now zigzags down towards a small creek. It does not go all the way down to it, however, but turns left, soon passing the mouth of the creek. When it reaches the quarry mentioned in the following note, you are offered a choice of ways down to the foreshore at Turnaware Point.** The one we took - the middle of three - passed close to what looked like the concrete base of one of the Nissen huts also mentioned in the note.

Turnaware Creek

TURNAWARE

The concrete road which brought you here is similar to one which runs to the "Smugglers' Cottage" at Tolverne from just above the King Harry Ferry, and another which goes down to Polgwidden Cove beach near Trebah on the Helford. Like those, this was built to enable US troops, tanks and other military vehicles to reach an embarkation point for the D-Day landings in Normandy in June 1944. The road to Turnaware, built by Irish navvies, was considered too narrow by the Americans when they arrived, and the black soldiers added six feet to its width "in no time at all". Once the road was built, the beach had to be prepared, as described in "Operation Cornwall" (by Viv Acton and Derek Carter, Landfall Publications 1994):

"Frank Curnow was appointed supervisor for the initial preparation for the beach at Turnaware Bar. He worked in the granite quarries at Porthoustock on the Lizard and was experienced in blasting, which was necessary on the rocky shore of the Bar. His work, with a small team, lasted from October 1943 until the following February, blasting, opening up a small quarry for hardcore, laying and then levelling the beach with a steam roller (caught on one occasion in the rising tide), and making the surface ready for the concrete 'matting' that would be placed on top. At the start of each week a lorry from Porthoustock Quarries came over the King Harry Ferry bringing dynamite, and collected the team on Friday evenings to take them back home for the week-end.

"The surfacing of the beach was carried out by the London firm of Harbour and General using flexible 'matting' made up of sections of concrete pads reinforced with steel wire. This provided the hard surface necessary for heavy vehicles. Nowadays some of these mats can be seen paving local farmyards or forming garden walls, as at Tolverne." Two photos in the same book (page 110) show that some of this "matting" is still in place at Turnaware, though it may be buried under shingle at times.

At Turnaware, the hard extended into the woodland beside the beach, as you will discover if you walk in: the trees thus provided camouflage for parked vehicles and other equipment in case of aerial attack. Nissen huts, iron ammunition stores and gunsites were also positioned among the trees, and the concrete bases for some of these can still be found.

Two "dolphins" (jetties) had to be constructed at Turnaware, using long iron or timber piles linked by iron gangways: see "Operation Cornwall" pages 111-3 and "Cornish War & Peace" pages 156-7; the two big chunks of concrete with protruding rusty girders on the foreshore at Turnaware are relics of these. One is seen in the sketch below.

9 The concrete road soon brings you back to the main entrance to the National Trust property. Immediately before you reach it the concrete road

Picnic at Turnaware Point

widens out into what was presumably a parking and/or turning space; notice on the left side the granite pillar commemorating the departure from Turnaware early in June 1944 of units of the 29th Infantry Division of the US Army, landing on D-Day at Omaha Beach, Normandy.

Retrace your steps from there to the parking place at the junction with the public road, where the footpath to St Just begins via a kissing gate.

10 The path at first heads gently downhill towards a distant stand of five pine trees, and soon runs close beside the woodland on your left. After a slightly marshy patch you pass among mature trees, continuing via a gate through attractive woodland. (See the photograph on the back cover.) On emerging into the open, go on in roughly the same line, down to the stile and footbridge at the head of St Just Creek. You are now back at point 2 on the map. Retrace your earlier steps back to the church, keeping close to the waterside all the way.

WALK 10

ST JUST AND ST MAWES

Between five and a half and seven and a half miles: see next page. Two shorter walks are suggested: one (about 2½ miles) omitting St Mawes, the other (about 4 miles) omitting St Just. For the latter, see the end of the main directions.

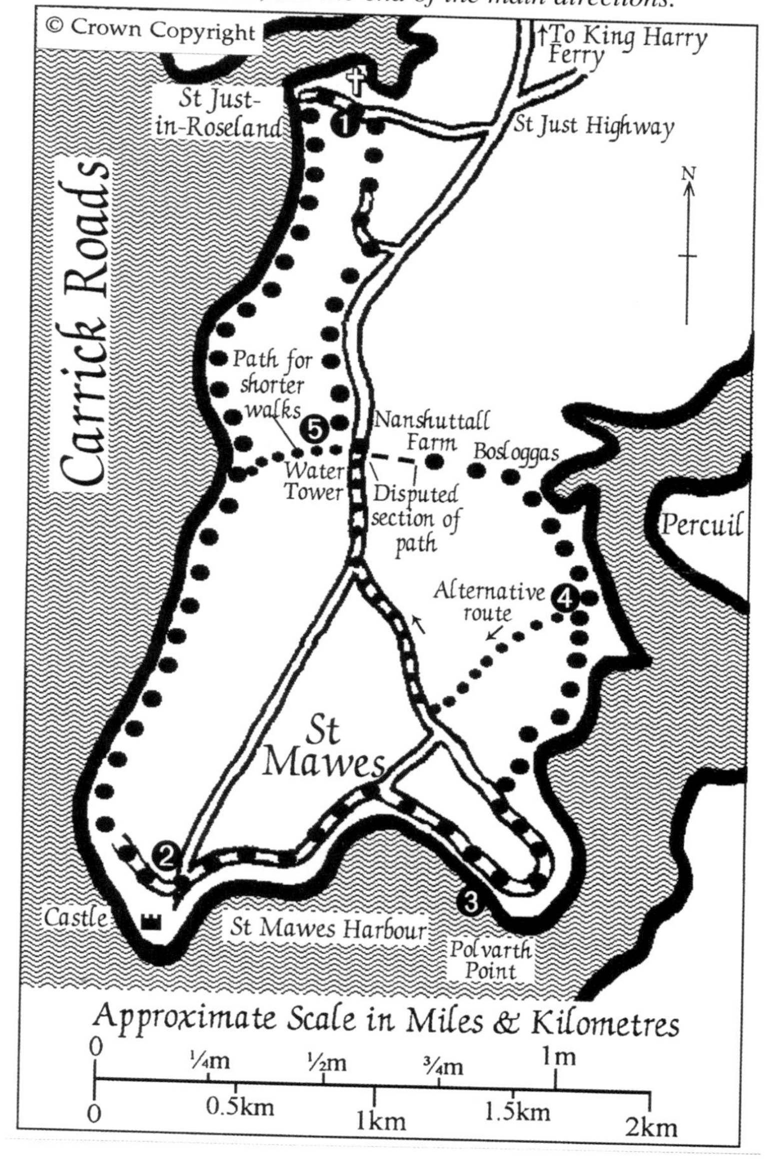

WALK 10

Of all the walks around the Fal that I know, I think this one most nearly approaches my notion of The Perfect Walk. (Its strongest rivals are Walks 9 and 12; which I prefer generally depends on which I did last!) What I called "one fly in the ointment" when I was writing the original *Around the Fal* has been removed: the right of way through one very short section at Nanshuttall Farm was in dispute then, but appears to have been finally accepted by the owners. Just in case the problem resurfaces, however, in the following directions and on the sketch map I also indicate an alternative way. For up-to-date information, ring the Cornwall County Council Highways Department (01209-820611, Extension 7239). Incidentally, the alternative way, though longer and less attractive, is worth knowing about, because the path approaching Nanshuttall is still not very well maintained, despite a few recent improvements: there's a very rickety little footbridge, for example.

The walk starts at probably the most famous small church in Cornwall and continues along the eastern shore of Carrick Roads - wonderful walking here, through gently rolling sheep-pasture; you then have a chance to look over St Mawes Castle - see page 97 for opening times - before visiting St Mawes (very conveniently placed for "facilities" and refreshments); next comes lovely creek scenery; and finally a ridgetop path with, along with those on parts of Walk 9, probably the most spectacular views to be had anywhere around the Fal - and that's a big claim to make. If the weather is right for bathing, there are several suitable beaches along the way, some of which are likely to be deserted except perhaps at the very height of the season. Some parts of the path will be muddy in wet periods; there are a large number of stiles to cross and a few hills to climb, but nothing frightening.

There is a convenient free - though rather small - car park at St Just-in-Roseland Church.

ROSELAND

As the map-maker John Norden wrote in 1584: "The peninsula is called by the pretty name of 'Roseland' which has, however, nothing to do with flowers, being derived from 'Rhos', the Celtic word for heath or gorse." Explanations of Cornish place-names are often controversial, though, and you may prefer another scholar's interpretation of "ros" as "a point extending into the sea". In any case, gorse is usually in bloom, so even "heathland" does have something to do with flowers!

Directions to King Harry Ferry from Truro and Falmouth are given at the start of Walk 11. Once you have crossed into the Roseland, follow signs to St

Mawes, and when you reach the small village known as St Just Highway watch for the right turning to the church. There is (2002) a bus service linking Truro, St Just and St Mawes and St Austell, namely First No.51/51A: see current timetables.

If you are coming from Falmouth you may prefer to use the passenger ferry to St Mawes, which operates all year except on Sundays out of season (November to March). In that case you would pick up the walk directions at the bottom of page 98. For information about the Falmouth - St Mawes ferry service, ring 01326 - 313813 (November to March) or 01326- 313201 (April to October).

ST JUST-IN-ROSELAND

Whether you find St Just Church an inspiring place perhaps depends on whether you agree that

> *"You are nearer God's heart in a garden*
> *Than anywhere else on earth."*

Each time I go I prepare myself to be repelled by the element of kitsch in and around the famous graveyard, with its carefully directed streams, rather twee carved quotations, and every inch beautified by the gardeners (John Betjeman's

St Just-in-Roseland Church
Gales have brought down some of the trees since this drawing was made.

verdict is: "It is the ideal resting place for lovers of 'Forest Lawn' in America and Woking in Surrey"); but each time I am bowled over by the sheer magic of the setting and the simple charm of the church itself, tucked down so low by the water that from the top of the churchyard you look down on the top of the tower. The building dates from the 13th century and was restored during the 19th by the architect who also redesigned St Anthony Church, and who seems to have been more sensitive to the spirit of the original buildings than many of his contemporaries were.

1 From the church take the path to the left, close to the creekside. You might care to go down to the foreshore below the path and walk to the right among the boats out on to St Just Bar, where you have a good view of the narrow entrance to St Just Creek. **After Pasco's boatyard - already in business at least a century ago, and still using traditional methods of boatbuilding and repair - keep right, following the sign to St Mawes, and bear left at Bar Point house. The path goes to the left of a bungalow. Cross the stile and from there the path keeps close to the edge of the low cliff all the way to St Mawes,** giving fine views of Carrick Roads.

CARRICK ROADS

This is the deep-water anchorage for Falmouth Harbour and Docks and towns up-river such as Penryn and Truro. It is said to be the world's third largest natural harbour, after Sydney and Rio de Janeiro. "Rode" would be a more logical spelling, because the word refers to the ability of ships to ride out storms here, or simply to ride at anchor. The water depth varies greatly, from about four feet at low tide north of Mylor to about a hundred feet at the seaward end. The word "Carrick" derives from the Cornish "garrak", rock, and refers to Black Rock at the entrance to the Roads; this was previously called "an garrak ruen", Seal Rock. Hilary Thompson tells me that seals still congregate there at low water.

Occasionally a gate or stile by the edge of the low cliff gives you a chance to go down on to the foreshore, where you could walk along the sand and do a little rock-scrambling, if the tide is low enough, as a change from the upper path.

To shorten the walk to about 2½ miles, omitting St Mawes, follow the sign, "Public Bridleway, St Mawes Garage". This comes just before a stile about a mile south of St Just. (As a further guide to help you recognise

the correct point, there is a National Trust sign, Newton Cliff, immediately beyond the stile.) About 20 yards after turning left, go right up a grassy track, then immediately left, following the red arrow on a post.

This quite steep path must, I think, be what remains of a lane mentioned by Laurence O'Toole as running down from the high road to the White House Inn, which stood, along with a malt house, a brewing house and a lime kiln, beside a small quay in a sheltered little cove. (See *The Roseland*, page 145.)

The path reaches the road close to a water tower. To return to St Just, cross the stile on the left and continue the directions from point 5.

For the full walk, continue by the water. Eventually, a gate brings you on to a road at the edge of St Mawes, and now you have your first good view of Falmouth Bay to the right and St Anthony Lighthouse to the left. In front is St Mawes Castle. Its opening times are: 10 am to 6 pm April to September; 10 am to 4 pm rest of year. It is closed for lunch from 1 to 2 pm. From 1 November to 31 March the castle is closed on Mondays and Tuesdays.

ST MAWES AND ST MAWES CASTLE

Prehistoric remains suggest that there was a settlement and fortress here in pre-Christian times, and that tin was exported from St Mawes in the Bronze Age. The village is named after St Maudetus, a 5th-century Breton or Irish religious teacher. An alternative name for the village in early times was Lavausa or Lavowsa, meaning "church-site of Mausa"; later on, however,

Lavausa was the smaller of two manors whose estates included what we now know as St Mawes. The other manor was Bogullas.

The castle, unusually designed in the form of a clover-leaf as seen from above, dates from 1543, and is one of three Henry VIII planned to build to guard Carrick Roads, Penryn, Truro and Tregony: see the notes on Pendennis Castle (Walk 1) and Flushing (Walk 2). Attack from the landward side was never expected, so during the Civil War its Royalist governor capitulated immediately when Fairfax threatened it in March 1646. The threat it faced in 1881 was at least as dramatic: the Morley report of that year recommended its demolition on the grounds that "it has little or no value as a work of defence against modern artillery." Rather grudgingly, however, the report added that "it forms an object of great historical interest, and great local objections exist to its removal."

In 1562 St Mawes was given the right to elect two MPs - "more by favour than by merit", remarked Richard Carew (1555-1620) in his Survey of Cornwall - so it was one of the notorious "Rotten Boroughs" which were disenfranchised in 1832. In fact the only burgesses with the right to vote were those of Lavausa manor, fewer than fifty men in all.

Not much is left now of the old fishing village, which in 1826 had ten seines employing a total of 155 men: St Mawes became one of Cornwall's most fashionable small resorts early this century, and most of the waterfront area - formerly the province of netmakers, chandlers, fish cellars and other maritime industries among the whitewashed cottages - was transformed as a result. Two photographs in Peter Gilson's "The Lower Fal" (p. 16) show something of this transformation, with the Ship and Castle Hotel dominating the quay in the post-1900 picture. Both photographs, however, show one very curious feature, a wall built right across the quayside road, with a door which was locked at night. it seems that the wall marked the boundary between the estates of Lavausa manor and those of a smaller tenement called Bohella to the east. Lavausa owned the harbour pier and claimed the harbour dues plus all the local fishing and anchorage rights, so its territory must have been worth defending. It's tempting to imagine St Mawes as the setting for a Cornish "West Side Story", with angry parents threatening to disinherit their son for courting an "extramural" girl ..

2 After passing the castle, follow the road right through the village, past the Idle Rocks Hotel. Notice the mesembryanthemums (Livingstone daisies) growing on the small cliff just after the hotel.

3 **Just before a group of pine trees there is a path down to the beach. If the tide is low enough you could take this and walk round Polvarth Point on the foreshore, so long as you don't mind scrambling over rocks and stepping over mooring ropes.** Three pilchard cellars once stood beside the foreshore close to Polvarth Point; the cellars have gone now, but the quays that served them survive. (A fascinating advertisement for the auction of the property of the Trusty Sean at Polvarth Cellars in 1851 is reproduced on page 99 of O'Toole's *The Roseland*.) **Continue past the St Mawes Sailing Club, situated on the old Stoneworks Quay, and when you reach a boatyard turn left and follow the footpath signposted "Porthcuel Creek".**

Or, if you keep to the road past the pine trees, take the lane on your right immediately before Freshwater Lane; it is signed "Polvarth Boatyard". The signed footpath to Porthcuel Creek is on the left at the bottom.

Whichever route you take, at the start you will get a good view of Place House on the opposite shore. There is a note about it in Walk 12. Polvarth Boatyard was owned for over 200 years by the Peters family, well known for the pilot gigs they used to build, and much more recently for the St Mawes One Design sailing boat, the invention of Frank Peters (1902-95). The boatyard was transformed during World War 2 to enable it to convert and maintain launches for the D-Day landings.

The path goes left behind another boatyard; turn right at the lane, and as you approach the bottom take the narrow, gravelled path on the left, which runs beside and behind a new-looking (in 2002) wooden building. Now continue along the waterside again. At the entrance to a field there is (or was, again in 2002) an awkward bit of fence to negotiate: too high to climb over easily, and too low for many people to duck under. Having solved that problem, keep to the hedge on your right at first, and then cut across the field past a tree with a yellow waymark arrow on a wooden post beneath it. The path goes on uphill, between bramble clumps to the left of several trees.

4 **At the top of the slope, where the field ends, you will find two footpath signs, one pointing left and the other, labelled Porthcuel, right.**

My preferred route from this point is to take the right turning: this is by far the more attractive way, considerably shorter than the alternative, and cuts out a quite lengthy stretch of road walking. I must warn you, though, that parts of the path are at present not well maintained: it may be somewhat overgrown and/or muddy and slippery in places; there is some mild scrambling to do at one point, where a small stream is crossed; and at least one footbridge and one stile are in urgent need of replacement. If nevertheless you decide to try this route, skip the next paragraph and follow the directions after that.

For the longer alternative, take the path on the left. You will soon pass through a kissing gate. The official path crosses the centre of the field. When you reach some granite steps into the next field, cross them and follow straight on, keeping the hedge to your right. (If you look back, you will see that the road from Percuil on the other side of the creek follows in a straight line from the path you're on. In "the old days" this was the usual route from St Mawes to the Percuil ferry.) **Another kissing gate brings you to houses; turn left and bear left again, then right on to the main road - rather busy, I'm afraid. Continue on this for about half a mile, eventually passing a water tower on your left. Now pick up the directions at point 5.**

For the other route, via Bosloggas and Nanshuttall Farm, follow the sign down the steepish path to the right, ignore the garden gate ahead, and go up to the left behind a wooden building. You are now opposite Percuil (see Walk 11), at the point where there was once a ferry service.

You next enter another field. Keep by the right edge, and soon you will come down to the pretty little inlet at Bosloggas.

Bosloggas house, which you can glimpse on your right a little later, was for a time the Cornish home of the millionaire Peter de Savary.

Follow the green arrow down to the stream (easier said than done, unless things have improved: this is where the "mild scrambling" was necessary). **Cross the small wooden stile in the barbed-wire fence on the far side of the stream, then climb the stone steps and walk up the valley.** The path keeps close to the stream; in spring and early summer it is delightful, with masses of comfrey and bluebells. Soon comes the plank footbridge I mentioned earlier: unless it has been replaced or repaired since I was last there, you will need to tread with great care. A little further on is another wooden footbridge - much more substantial, but also starting to look as if it needs attention. A muddy patch further up the valley has been provided with a few planks doing duty as stepping-stones, but these tend to be slippery. **When you reach a substantial wooden stile, cross it and turn left towards the farm buildings. Before you reach them there is a farm gate. This is where the right of way used to stop, according to the owners of the farm, but now you should be able to go on ahead through the farmyard and along the farm drive, emerging at the road almost opposite a water tower. Turn right on the road.**

5 Cross the stile on the left just past the water tower, following the sign to St Just. The path, created by the National Trust, keeps beside the field edge on the right, close to the road, and includes several well-made stiles. The view along here is breathtaking - my drawing ranging over four pages at the front of this book is an attempt to illustrate it - and every few yards of walking seems to reveal new aspects of it.

Eventually you reach a lane, where you follow the sign to the left. The lane becomes a track and finally a path, often rather churned up by the cattle of Churchtown Farm. After passing among a few houses, you reach the road opposite the church's upper lychgate, and from here it is pleasant to walk back to the car park through the Memorial Gardens on the right, rather than along the road. Alternatively, go down to the church again, and then it's worth stepping over the cattle grid in the lower lychgate on the right and strolling a little way along the path beside the creek, which gives you lovely views of the church.

SHORT WALK, OMITTING ST JUST

Just under four miles (via Nanshuttall Farm)

Starting at the main car park in St Mawes, turn left at the sea-front, go past the Idle Rocks Hotel, and then follow the directions from point 3. At point 5, go down the bridleway signed to Carrick Roads instead of crossing the stile. You walk along a field-edge at first, but when this curves left there is a slightly sunken path between hedges. A few years ago this tended to be rather overgrown, but it seems to be kept in good order nowadays. Turn left at the bottom to return to St Mawes.

WALK 11

PORTH, PORTSCATHO & PERCUIL

About six miles.

Walks 11 and 12 could be combined, so the map is at the start of Walk 12. For two shorter walks, omitting the coast, see the end of the directions.

The last two walks, like the first, include some sea coast in contrast to river and creek. This one begins with a gentle section of the South Cornwall Coastal Footpath which has extensive views across Gerrans Bay to the Dodman; next comes an attractive fishing village, with its mother church a little way inland and on top of a hill at Gerrans (quite similar to Gorran Churchtown in relation to Gorran Haven - which is just one of the two reasons why I tend to confuse Gerrans and Gorran!). After the short inland walk come peaceful, secluded creeks, skirted for the most part by a well-made path provided by the National Trust. There is little road walking involved, and mud is not usually too much of a problem on the paths, but three short sections of path are very steep (one down, two up) and likely to be slippery. Portscatho has shops, a good pub and other facilities, conveniently placed at about the half-way point. There are also seasonal toilets at Porth, where the walk starts and ends, and at Percuil.

Park at the National Trust car park at Porth Farm (Grid Reference: SW 868 329). To get there from Truro or Falmouth, take the A39 as far as the Playing Place double roundabout, which is between Truro and Carnon Downs. Follow signs from there to King Harry Ferry. Except at very busy times, when it tends to set off as soon as it is full, the ferry operates every 20 minutes, apart from Sundays in winter: it leaves on the hour, then at 20 past and 20 to the hour from the near (Trelissick) side, and ten minutes later than those times from the Philleigh side. After the crossing, follow signs to St Mawes at first. Nearly two miles along the road, take the left turn, following signs to Gerrans. At Gerrans take the road signposted St Anthony Head. About a mile later you pass the head of a creek on your right, and the car park is on your right soon after that, clearly signed by the National Trust.

Bus service 51/51A links Truro, Portscatho and St Mawes: see current timetables. To start the walk in Portscatho, pick up the directions at point 2.

1 Take the path marked "Beach" opposite the car park entrance. (Seasonal toilets are in the building you pass through here.) **The coast path heading towards Portscatho goes off to the left just before you reach the beach (Towan). It is clearly marked all the way to the village.** As mentioned near the start of Walk 12, the lane down to Towan Beach was originally used by farmers as a cart track for bringing up seaweed and sand to spread on the fields. Hilary Thompson tells me there were six such "sanding roads" between Towan and Portscatho; as you walk you might care to try to work out where they must have been. Somewhere near Greeb or Grebe Point there is a sailor's grave, marked by two upright stones sunk in the ground on the edge of the cliff, six feet apart, but it takes a keen eye to spot the place. Once you have passed the Point you have good views of Gerrans Bay, with Carne Beacon and Pendower Beach prominent to the left of Nare Head, and Gull Rock (one of many so named: "Nine, to be precise," says Peter Gilson) off to the right. The church spire is that of Gerrans. Spires are quite rare on Cornish churches, and the few that were erected seem usually to have been intended as landmarks to guide navigation. This one is said to have been built at the request of fishermen in the 15th century.

GERRANS

The name is pronounced with a hard G, and is apparently derived from "St Gerent" or "Geraint" or "Gerennins", King of Cornwall from 580 to 586 A.D. Despite a serious fire in the middle of last century which made extensive rebuilding necessary, the church still has many early features, such as a Norman font, 15th-century granite arches and some Tudor bench ends.

Soon after entering Portscatho you pass the Post Office on your right, and then the pub (The Plume of Feathers) before reaching The Square with its various shops.

PORTSCATHO

The name is from Cornish: "landing-place of boats". Some guide books claim that the locals say it as "P'scatha" or just "Scatha", but Hilary Thompson's comment on that is, "Actually, we locals of many generations have never shortened the pronunciation, though I have heard visitors do so!" Farming has always been the main source of income - though the holiday trade may have overtaken it by now - but the pilchard fishery used to be very important. Laurence O'Toole quotes "an ancient Portscatho fisherman" as saying that up to about 1850 "under all the old houses there were fish cellars. ... They used to cure fish up as far as the Square." It was not fishing, though, but the merchant schooner trade which was chiefly responsible for the development of Portscatho in the mid-19th century: hence the preponderance of substantial terraced houses and "villas" in Portscatho rather than of fishermen's cottages as at Portloe and Mevagissey.

"From the Roseland to St Austell Bay" includes a fuller note on the village.

2 To continue the walk, return to the Post Office and take the footpath opposite, signposted Percuil.

3 At the top of the steep slope and steps, the path goes almost straight on (just slightly right). The first field you pass through was the site of a prehistoric burial mound. Early this century it was ploughed up, and the superstitious farm workers threw away the burial urn they found inside. **Make for the corner of a field surrounded by hedges on the left, and then still continue in a straight line till you reach a metal 7-bar gate. This brings you to a lane and soon to a road.**

4 Turn left, and soon right along a short stretch of track leading to an area where usually boats, black plastic farm bales etc etc are stored. On the right here is a stile (which, incidentally, is listed grade II) beside a gateway, giving access to a path signposted to Percuil. Now head for the nearest telegraph pole and then to the stile in the hedge, going straight on across the next field to another stile which brings you out on to another road. Continue along the road almost opposite, marked Portcuil. As you turn into this road, on the left you will see Parson's Pool, an old roadside pond which the local Old Cornwall Society has restored - though by 2002 it was so choked with vegetation as to be scarcely recognisable. Here on the left is the Victorian Rectory, now a private house, the site of the old parsonage.

5 On reaching the farm (Tregassick, "farm in a reedy place" according to Weatherhill), take the lane on your right, marked "National Trust - Footpath to Percuil 1m". (The sign, on the right side of the lane, may be partly hidden by leaves; the lane starts almost opposite the attractive, slate-hung Tregassick House.) Next, about 100 yards after passing the last farm building, turn right down the path signposted Polingey Creek. Go through the right-hand gate on to a rather narrow, grassy path between hedges. Just before the next gate, cross the stile on the left, go along the right side of the field, and then follow the yellow arrow to the right, over two stiles and down a steep path to Polingey Creek. (Although rough steps have been cut, this descent can still be a bit perilous in damp conditions - take care!)

The remains of a causeway across the creek are still clear, a few yards to the right of where the path comes down. This is a relic of a tide mill which was worked till the middle of the 19th century. It belonged to the very important Manor of Tregaire, about which some details are given in Walk 1 of *From the Roseland to St Austell Bay*. The mill and house stood on the mound in the middle with high causeways on either side. The name Polingey (like Bolingey, near Perranporth) derives from the Cornish, *melyn-jy*, mill house.

6 Turn left and follow the footpath beside the water (or mud, if the tide's out) around to Percuil.

An aerial photo by P. Strings of Percuil Creek. Just left of centre is Percuil Boatyard. There is a glimpse of the sea top-right.

PERCUIL

The name, probably meaning "the narrow harbour", is pronounced with the stress on the middle syllable: P'cuil, or even as two syllables: P'cule. Variant spellings include Porthcuel and Portcuil.

Although Percuil is still used by a few fishing vessels, it is now a centre for pleasure boats. There were fish cellars here in Tudor times, and till well into this century it was an important trading-port, benefiting from a channel with 6 feet of water at low tide and 24 at high: lime and South American guano for fertilizer were brought by small boats, and coal by bigger ones. Up to 1939 a steam ferry operated between here and Falmouth, and till about 1948 a rowing-boat ferry provided a link with St Mawes. Laurence O'Toole mentions that even before any ferry existed Percuil seems to have been a crossing-point: a stony bar that still survives may have originated as a man-made causeway, "and," he adds, "one may still walk it, waist deep on the lowest tides." I have not put his assertion to the test.

Peter Gilson's "The Lower Fal" has four photographs showing various cargoes being unloaded from ketches, schooners and barges into carts at Percuil. The quaint cottages, mostly thatched, surrounding the slipway and foreshore - one of them originally the Passage Inn - bear little resemblance to the modern premises of Percuil Boat Yard, described by Peter as "a functional concrete monstrosity".

From the car park, it's worth turning right to look at the boatyard at the former ferry point; then return up the road past the car park. A few yards past the upper car park entrance, cross the stile on the right, signposted Pelyn Creek and Trewince Avenue.

From the bench as you approach the creek you have a view south-west along the Percuil River to the outskirts of St Mawes. It's also an excellent vantage point for birdwatching: as I sat there having my picnic lunch on one occasion, I saw - apart from the many usual waders and gulls - at least two hawks and up to a dozen herons. The latter appeared to be nesting in the trees on the far side of the creek.

7 At the head of Pelyn Creek you have to turn inland.

The name Pelyn, sometimes spelt Polyn, probably means something similar to Penpol, "head-pool" or "creek-head".

First follow the sign right to Trewince Avenue, cross the stream (if a stream exists: in a dry summer it probably doesn't) and the stile to the left, then walk up by the field edge on your left. Cross the stile on the left by the house and then, after about ten yards, go up the steep, narrow and possibly rather overgrown path on the right, marked by a yellow arrow on a wooden post. After a little gate, go along the right edge of the field for a few yards, then through the gap ahead (crossed now by a wooden fence whose top bar lifts), on to a farm track. When you reach the concreted farmyard turn left along a wide farm lane.

8 At the road (where Trewince Avenue begins, its trees replanted in November 1992 to mark the 40th anniversary of the Queen's accession to the throne), **go straight on, passing the entrance to Trewince Manor Holiday Estate and Restaurant.** From this point there is a fine coastal view taking in both Nare Head and the Dodman.

TREWINCE

Trewince (Cornish: "homestead in the wind") was the home of several generations of "squires", the last of them being the Thomas family. Trewince

Manor is ancient, but the present house dates from about 1750. Trewince Avenue, which ran from the entrance to Trewince for about a quarter of a mile along the almost straight road towards Gerrans, is mentioned by the Radford sisters (see the note about them in Walk 12) in their autobiography: "... the green of the leafy tunnel in summer, and in winter the silhouette of the branches almost meeting, cathedral-like, across the aisle of the narrow road." It was lined with elms and was said to be haunted by a lady searching for buried treasure. The elms were presumably victims of Dutch elm disease; some of their stumps remain. Whether the ghost still lurks among the eighty new saplings I don't know.

Soon you pass beside Froe Creek and come back to the car park at Porth Farm. You can avoid walking on the road for these last few hundred yards by taking the pretty footpath on the right.

FROE

The largest house to be seen at Froe now was once the mill: there was a tide mill here, and the pool is clearly separated from the creek by a causeway. An advertisement in 1809 offered for sale "Newbuilt dwelling house and water grist mills called Frow mills." Until the early 20th century, Froe was quite a busy little port: small boats brought in coal and collected flour from the mill.

Porth Creek on a rainy day

Froe Creek almost makes an island of St Anthony parish, and the neck of land between Froe and Towan Beach is so narrow that in storms sea-spray can sometimes be felt here.

SHORTER WALKS

Just under and just over four miles

A pleasant walk can be made by taking the footpath north from Porth Farm to Froe and continuing along the road as far as Tregassick Farm. The road, including Trewince Avenue, is usually quiet, despite some holiday traffic in the summer, and from parts of it you have good coastal views. To get to Tregassick Farm, after a little over a mile take the left turning signposted Portcuil, which is referred to towards the end of section 4 in the main walk directions. From there, follow the directions from point 5 onwards for the waterside walk back to Porth Farm.

Another possibility, slightly longer but avoiding nearly all the road walking, is to use the bridleway/footpath which starts as a track on the right a few yards north of the car park at Porth Farm. Despite the high, flower-filled hedges you get a few good views to the left early on, taking in Froe Creek, Percuil Creek and St Mawes. Where the lane bends left, continue ahead (blue arrow) and cross a stile. If the course of the path in the field beyond is not obvious, head towards the largest barn. Cross another wooden stile, and then as you approach the farm buildings cross the stone stile on your right. Turn left on the lane, passing beside the fine old house of Rosteague, which is part-Elizabethan and part-Georgian. Beyond Rosteague you continue north towards Gerrans on the long entrance drive to the house. After rather more than half a mile you will join a minor road, eventually reaching the buildings of Treloan Farm, where you should turn left and cross the stile, joining the path signposted to Percuil. This is the one mentioned in the first few lines of section 4; follow the main directions for the rest of the walk.

WALK 12

PORTH & ST ANTHONY IN ROSELAND

About six miles - or see the end of the directions for a version about half that length starting at St Anthony Head. Walks 11 and 12 could be combined.

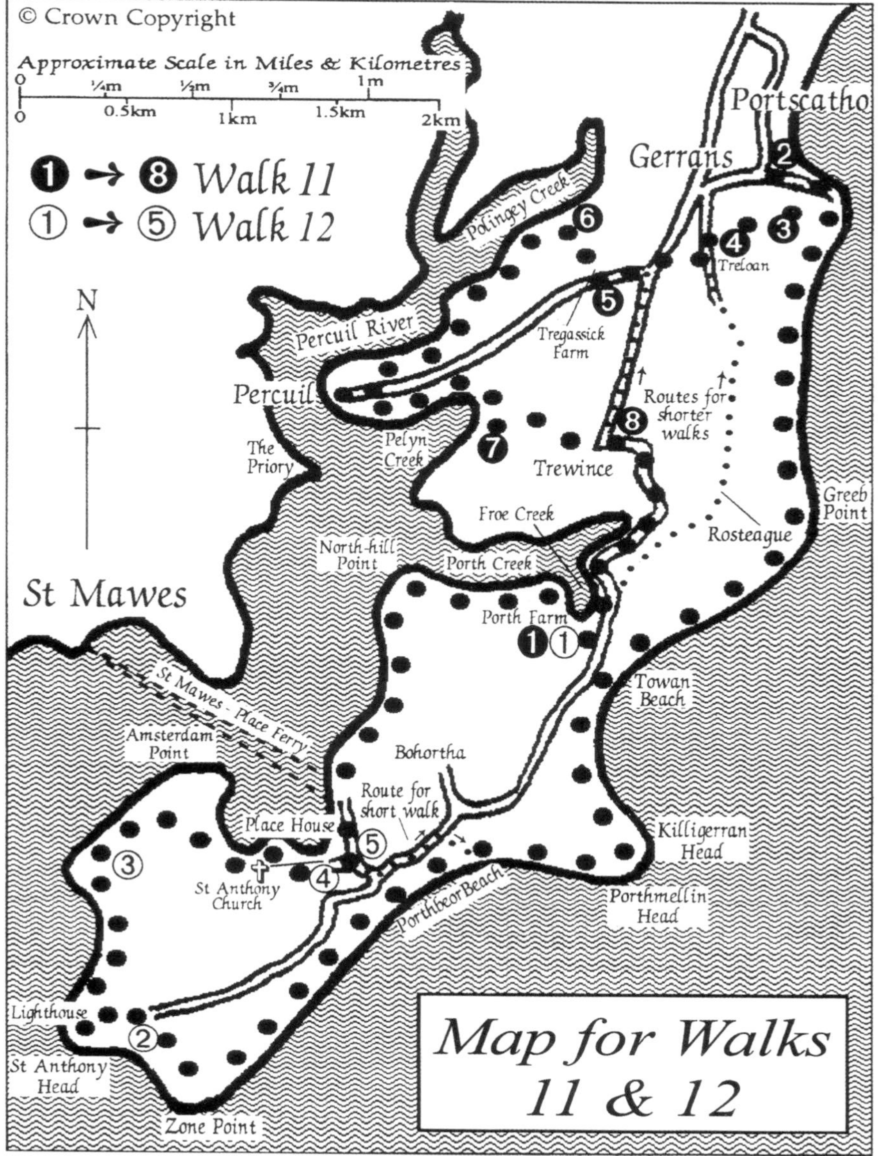

WALK 12

Yet another walk of great beauty and variety: it vies, I think, with Walks 9 and 10 for the title of the most magnificent walk "around the Fal". It includes not only lush creekside settings and panoramic views of Falmouth Harbour and St Mawes, but also some rocky cliffs - hardly spectacular, perhaps, but a dramatic contrast to the soft riverside slopes which in places are only a few hundred yards away across the peninsula. You also pass a large country house in a superb setting, an interesting little Norman church, and a lighthouse which is often open for visits. The path is well marked most of the way and is not usually very muddy. Toilets are available at both Porth and St Anthony Head, but there is no pub, café or shop anywhere along the route, the nearest ones being at Gerrans and Portscatho.

If you are interested in recent military history, it would be a good idea to bring with you one or both of the booklets mentioned in the italicised note on St Anthony Battery, although quite a lot of basic information is now provided at the site.

Parking for the shorter walk: see page117; for the longer one, park at Porth Farm. (Directions to Porth are given for Walk 11.)

Alternatively, during the summer months (May to September inclusive) you could use the St Mawes - Place ferry, which would enable you to do either the full walk or the shorter route, starting partway through point 5 in the directions. The normal pattern is that this ferry runs every half hour from 10 am to 4.30 pm from St Mawes and 15 minutes later from Place, but there is no ferry at 1 pm (1.15 return). If you wish to enquire about the ferry service, telephone 01209-214901. It would of course be possible to come to Place from Falmouth using both the ferries: see the introduction to Walk 10 for some information about the Falmouth-St Mawes ferry service.

There is no bus service that would be useful for this walk.

1 Take the path marked "Beach" almost opposite the car park entrance. (Seasonal toilets are in the building you pass through here.) The lane that runs down to Towan Beach is a reminder of the former importance of seaweed as a fertiliser: Laurence O'Toole quotes an account written early in the 19th century of the way all the local farmers would converge with their carts on Towan at every spring tide and after every southerly gale to gather the ore weed. "Towan" means sandhill; although the narrow neck of land between here and Froe consists, says O'Toole, largely of windblown sand, dunes aren't much in evidence now, perhaps because those same farmers have raided them for sand to sweeten their acid soils.

Most people use one or other of the grassy paths leading towards the cliff edge; but if you take the lane, just before reaching the beach go up the path on your right on to the cliff. The Coast Path is very clear all the way round southwards from here past Killigerran Head, Porthmellin Head, Porthbeor Beach and Zone Point to St Anthony Head.

The prominent "Wreck Post" which you soon come to is one of several around the coast for use in life-saving exercises, as explained in some detail on a plaque attached to the post.

"Killigerran" or "Killygerran" means "the grove of Geraint": see the note on Gerrans in Walk 11. "Porthmellin" probably means "mill cove", but it's difficult to imagine a watermill on or near this headland; could it have been a windmill? Another possibility is that "mellin" here derives from Cornish *melyn*, yellow, and could refer to furze (gorse). Steps lead down to the beach at Porthbeor (meaning "big cove" and pronounced, I am told, "Polbare"). The cluster of houses you see to the right at this point is the hamlet of Bohortha (glossed as "cowyard" or "cowsheds" by Oliver Padel, but Hilary Thompson suggests "the higher house"). Originating as three farms close together, Bohortha in its heyday boasted an inn, a school, a smithy and probably also a bakery.

At the National Trust "Zone Point" sign, less than half a mile after Porthbeor, you get your first glimpse over the ridge of St Mawes, Falmouth Docks and Pendennis Castle, with the large house called Roseland Place in the foreground. This was originally called Little Place; it was built by the Spry family of Place for letting, but the Sprys moved into it when the big house was requisitioned in World War 2, and they stayed on there for many years afterwards. As you reach Zone Point (named from the Cornish word *sawn*, a cleft or gully) your view also extends along the coast westward to the Manacles. See the note about the lighthouse for information about them.

2 As you approach St Anthony Head, you pass through (or beside, depending which route you take) the remains of the St Anthony Battery.

ST ANTHONY BATTERY

Like Pendennis, St Anthony headland has been fortified since at least the Iron Age. The walls and ditches of the Iron Age cliff castle are hard to trace now, but you can hardly fail to notice the substantial remains of fortifications placed here during the past century or so. The oldest date from the 1890s, although a small earthen battery had been set up as early as 1805. The battery was re-equipped and fully manned during both World Wars: O'Toole refers to "as many as three thousand troops at a time" living in tents there during World War 1. It was not finally abandoned by the military until 1956, three years before the National Trust took over the site. Detailed descriptions and explanations of the St Anthony Battery are given in two cheap and easily portable publications, a "Coast of Cornwall" leaflet prepared for the National Trust by the South Cornwall Heritage Coast Project, and Jeff Dorman's "The Later Defences of Falmouth". A windfall courtesy of the National Lottery has, since I originally researched this walk, enabled more parts of the battery to be restored, access to be improved, and helpful signs and notices to be provided.

Soon afterwards - just as you reach the National Trust car park - be careful not to miss the path down to the left, signed to the Rampart, Battery, Observation Post and Bird Hide. A little way down, keep right, following the sign to St Anthony Lighthouse, and eventually turn sharp-right at the acorn sign to continue with the coastal footpath.

ST ANTHONY LIGHTHOUSE

The lighthouse was built in 1834-5. Many people have always maintained that it ought to have been set on top of the hill rather than down by the water, since despite the fact that the theoretical range of its light is 22 miles, owing to the curvature of the earth it can be seen no more than 10 miles away (or 14, according to some sources) to the south and west, and not at all to the east. There was no fog-warning device at the lighthouse until 1882, when a bell weighing two tons - the biggest in Cornwall - was installed; it was eventually superseded by an automatic fog-horn in 1954. The lighthouse is now fully automated, and is run by a man-and-wife team, so opening times for visits cannot be regular, but you may well be lucky. Its light, supplied by a 1500-watt bulb, shines red in the direction of the Manacles. This is a notorious group of submerged and half-submerged rocks about half way between Falmouth and Lizard Point: the reef stretches a mile and a half out to sea and is two miles wide. The Manacles have been the cause of many a wreck, probably the best-known of which was that of the 'Mohegan' in 1898. Their name means Church Rocks (maen eglos): the church spire at St Keverne has traditionally been used as a landmark to help sailors to avoid them.

The path gives you fine views across to Pendennis as you pass among a group of windswept pines, and then of St Mawes castle and village.

Looking back to the St Anthony lighthouse

3 As you approach the patch of woodland at Amsterdam Point, you have to turn right and climb the hill. Cross the hedge where the granite steps are, or follow the more obvious path through gateways, and continue down towards Place House. The path takes you beside Cellars Beach (the name recalling pilchard cellars, where literally millions of fish were salted and packed in barrels) **and then behind the house, to the right.**

PLACE HOUSE

This stands on the site of a tiny Augustinian priory, built by the monks of Plympton in the 12th century. As at Froe and Polingey, the tidal waters here were impounded to drive a millwheel; this tidemill appears on Boazio's map (1597), and it was still working in 1848. Finally it was destroyed in 1860 when the millpool was turned into the lawn we now see in front of the house. When the monasteries were dissolved, about 1536-9, the stones from Place priory were taken by barge to St Mawes as building material for the new castle. Soon after, a large house (Cornish, "plas", mansion) was built here, bought by the Vyvyan family in Elizabeth I's reign and by the Spry family in the mid 17th century. Little or nothing of the old house survived the Victorian rebuilding ("symmetrical Neo-Gothic at its least attractive" in the opinion of

Nikolaus Pevsner). During World War 2 it was commandeered by the Royal Navy: Cellars Beach then was surrounded by Nissen huts, and there were gun emplacements on the hill to the south-west of the house. In the immediate post-war years the house was a home for displaced Europeans. In 1949 it was converted into a holiday camp; later it became Place Manor Hotel; and since 1982 it has reverted to its old status as a private house, still the home of the Sprys.

Place House. Beyond the wall is the lawn on the site of the former millpool

4 Yellow arrows direct you along to St Anthony Church.

ST ANTHONY CHURCH

"St Anthony" is an Anglicisation of the name of an early Cornish king and martyr, St Entenin, to whom the church of St Anthony in Meneage is also dedicated. (See "Around the Helford", Walk 2.)

Apparently a Saxon church stood here originally. When the priory was dissolved, the nave of the 12th-century church was spared because it had been in use for public worship. In the 19th century, soon after Place House was rebuilt, the chancel was rebuilt to match as closely as possible the medieval

one, and a tower was added to imitate the one on the house. The South doorway, built of Caen stone, is genuine Norman. Notice the Lamb and Cross carving over the south door, sometimes rather fancifully mentioned as evidence that Christ as a child visited St Anthony in the company of his uncle, Joseph of Arimathea.

Despite the high proportion of Victorian work, Pevsner calls St Anthony Cornwall's best example of what churches must have been like in the 12th century.

After the church, go on till you reach a road, and then turn left, passing on your right what was in 1989 the tiny Place Shellfish Purification Plant. It appears to be disused now.

5 There is a kissing gate on the right opposite the curved sea wall in front of Place House, and immediately above the point where the St Mawes ferry lands at high tide. Go through it and turn left, following the sign to Porth Farm. You now reach perhaps the prettiest stretch of the whole walk, with woodland, open fields, fine views back to St Mawes and Pendennis Castles and ahead to Percuil, Porth Creek and Froe.

Just as you enter Drawlers Plantation (National Trust), steps lead down to the landing place used by the ferry at low water or mid-tide. (These are the ones referred to in Laurence O'Toole's footnote: "Now known as 'Totty's Steps' in honour of Colonel Totty of the West Yorkshire Regiment, who had them built during World War One. It became necessary because so many of his men returning from the pubs of St Mawes fell into the water at that point.")

If you have just arrived on the ferry, welcome to the walk, and please take the path to the left.

A seat not much further along, with a wonderful view back to St Mawes Castle and Falmouth Docks, was placed here in memory of Maisie and Evelyn Radford (1911-73).

THE RADFORD SISTERS

Maisie and Evelyn Radford were Devonians who fell in love with the St Anthony area as a result of many youthful holidays, eventually settled there soon after the end of the First World War, and became leading lights in the world of music, especially opera, not only locally but much further afield. Their autobiography, "Musical Adventures in Cornwall" (David and Charles, 1965), now out of print but not hard to find in local libraries and secondhand bookshops, makes delightful reading even for anyone with little interest in music. I enjoy their wry sense of humour and their ability to convey the "feel" of life in and around the Roseland during those decades (roughly 1920-1960). Many of their journeys along remote country lanes in ancient and temperamental cars were "adventures" of a non-musical sort; so too were some of their boat trips: "We would row back on a dark winter night, with only the black shape of the trees by the landing strip where the wood ended or the position of the stars - Orion striding over the hilltop - to show us where to pull in ... and feel our way up the fields under the chestnut trees, listening to the owls hooting and sometimes the long cry of the curlews."

A later seat is equally well placed at North-hill Point for the view across the entrance to Porth Creek and up the Percuil River. Quay Cottage is immediately opposite. The quay (Trewince Quay) served a lime kiln and pilchard cellar: the kiln has gone now, but the walled area to the left of the cottage is a relic of the cellar: see Hilary Thompson's *History of the Parish of Gerrans*, Part 2, page 40. The ugly modern building further off, on the same side of the river, is the store and workshop at Percuil. The small headland on the far shore, roughly opposite Quay Cottage, is called The Priory, but this appears to be a fairly modern name. In the 19th century there was a substantial quay there, together with a lime kiln and a malthouse.

After about another quarter of a mile you may (depending on the height of hedges and the density of foliage) get a good view of the wall dividing the little Froe Creek from Porth Creek. This is the best-preserved example of a former tide mill anywhere around the Fal estuary. See the note on Froe in Walk 11.

6 Cross the footbridge at Froe and take the wide path on your right, which leads back to the car park.

SHORT WALK

About three miles

Park at St Anthony Head, then follow directions 2, 3 and 4 above, but turn right at the road after St Anthony Church. Keep on along the road for about half a mile, ignoring the right turn to Anthony Head, and take the path on the right down to the Coast Path above Porthbeor Beach.

FURTHER READING

FALMOUTH

Bob Acton & Peter Gilson: *Enjoy Falmouth & Around* (Landfall, 1998; 2nd edition with updates, 2003)

Fisher Barham: *Old Cornwall in Camera: Falmouth* (Glasney Press, 1977)

Nicola Darling-Finan: *Images of Bygone Falmouth* (Breedon Books, 2001)

Bob Dunstan: *The Book of Falmouth & Penryn* (Barracuda, 1975)

Peter Gilson: *Falmouth in Old Photographs* (Alan Sutton, 1990)

David Mudd: *Home Along Falmouth & Penryn* (Bossiney Books, 1980)

James Whetter: *The History of Falmouth* (Dyllansow Truran, 1981)

PENRYN

June Palmer: *The People of Penryn in the Seventeenth Century* (Author, 1986)

June Palmer: *Penryn in the Eighteenth Century* (Author, 1991)

Rita Tregellas Pope (ed.): *Memories of Old Penryn* (Dyllansow Truran, 1983)

R.J.Roddis: *Penryn - The History of an Ancient Cornish Borough* (D. Bradford Barton, 1964)

Ernie Warmington: *Penryn* (old photographs etc) (Author, no date)

James Whetter: *The History of Glasney College* (Tabb House, 1988)

THE FAL IN GENERAL AND OTHER PLACES AROUND IT

History Around the Fal (5 books by the Fal History Group, published by Exeter University, 1980-90)

Viv & Bob Acton: *A History of Truro* (Landfall, 1997-2003) (3 volumes, the last of which is in preparation and will consist of walks in the city and district)

Viv Acton: *Life by the Fal - Years of Change at Point & Penpol* (Landfall, 1993)

Viv Acton & Derek Carter: *Operation Cornwall 1940-1944 & Cornish War & Peace* (Landfall, 1994/1995)

Sheila Bird: *Around the Waterways of the Fal* (Bird of Freedom, 1988)

John Bridger: *A Personal History of St Feock 1900-2000*

Roger Burrows: *Wildlife of the Fal Estuary* (Harbour Books, 1984)

Peter Gilson: *The Lower Fal in Old Photographs* (Alan Sutton, 1992)

Peter Gilson: *The Upper Fal in Old Photographs* (Alan Sutton, 1994)

Phyllis M.Jones:*The Bells of Truro* (Landfall, 1994) (Pre-war memories of Truro, Falmouth, St Mawes etc.)

Liz Luck: *South Cornish Harbours* (Nautical Books, 1988)

David Mudd: *Around and About the Fal* (Bossiney, 1989)

Laurence O' Toole: *The Roseland - between River and Sea* (Lodenek, 1978)

Chris Pollard: *Looking Back at Old St Mawes* (Author, 1994)

Maisie & Evelyn Radford: *Musical Adventures in Cornwall* (David & Charles, 1965)

Jeanette Ratcliffe: *Fal Estuary Historic Audit* (Cornwall Archaeological Unit, 1997)

Hilary Thompson: *A History o f Gerrans and Portscatho 1700-1830* (Author, 1991)

Hilary Thompson: *A History of the Parish of Gerrans 1800-1914:*
Part 1: *Farms and Farmers* (Author, 1994)
Part 2: *Mariners and Fishermen* (Author, 1995)

Many of the above publications are out of print, but most should be available through public libraries.

Landfall Walks Books' "best seller" - rivalled only by *Around the River Fowey* - this selection of magnificent walks includes several around Falmouth, visiting Swanpool, Maenporth, Budock, Mawnan Smith, Durgan, Port Navas, Constantine and Helford Passage, as well as Gweek and the north side of the Helford River.

The 2003 reprint, which includes brief updates and other revisions, is priced £3.99.

This is an "omnibus", bringing together most of the walks which originally appeared in two books, *Around Mevagissey* and *Around St Austell*. It covers the territory immediately east of that featured in *Around the Fal*, and includes Philleigh, Veryan, Gorran, Mevagissey, Pentewan and Charlestown as well as inland places such as Tregony, Grampound, St Stephen, Polgooth, Trewoon and St Blazey.

The 2001 reprint, with revisions, costs £4.95.

The main aim of this fully illustrated book is to tell the interesting story of Falmouth through three short walks. Most of the factual material has been supplied by Peter Gilson, an authority on the history of Falmouth and the Fal. There are also about 50 pages of other local information, with sections such as Art & Artists in Falmouth, Parking, Public Transport, Child-Friendly Falmouth, and much more. Walks in the surrounding area and ten car tours based on Falmouth are briefly described.

The 2003 reprint, again with revisions, costs £3.99.

MORE LANDFALL BOOKS

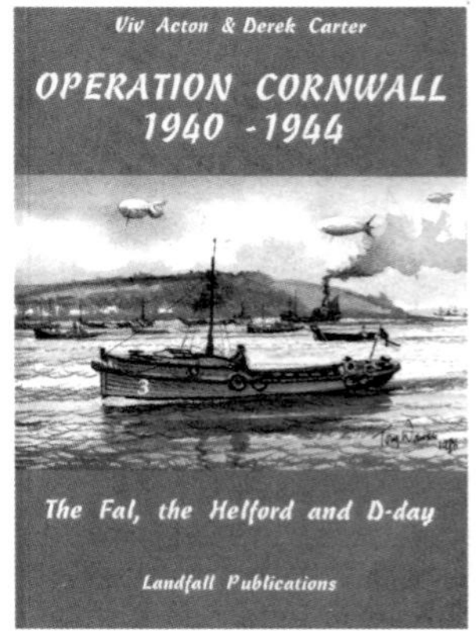

These two very popular books tell the story of Cornwall during World War 2. They focus, though not exclusively, on the Fal and Helford areas.

Price £6.99 each

These two books are detailed, fully illustrated guides to the Mineral Tramways Project routes (for walkers, cyclists and equestrians) between Portreath and Devoran and around Carn Brea.

Price £7.50 each

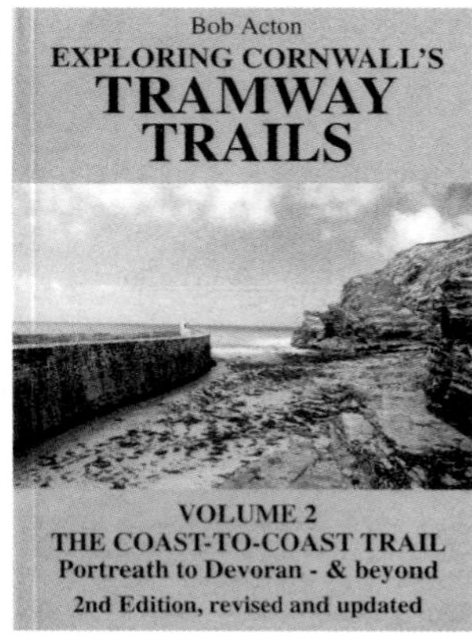

A history of this interesting district beside Restronguet Creek, once highly industrialised.

Price £4.95

These books and many others on Cornish topics are available in local bookshops and direct from

Landfall Publications
Landfall
Penpol
Devoran
Truro
Cornwall TR3 6NR
Telephone 01872 862581